Recovering from Redundancy

A guide to surviving a layoff and changing your life

ADRIAN WARNER

DEDICATION

To my father, who was made redundant in 1982, and
my mother for their wonderful upbringing and
support.

Adrian Warner

CONTENTS

Adrian Warner

ACKNOWLEDGEMENTS

I have spoken to many people about the challenges of redundancy in writing this book and I have decided not to use their names in order to protect their privacy. But I would like to thank them all for their honesty and cooperation.

In difficult times, we all cherish friendships and help and I would particularly like to thank Joanna Manning-Cooper, Kurt Barling, Tom Edwards, Victoria O'Byrne, Kate Ironside, Paul Rowinski, Ian Chadband, Jayne Pearce-McMenamin, Edward Simpson, Roger Weston and Neil Heydon-Dumbleton for their valuable guidance.

My singing with Crouch End Festival Chorus has been a wonderful tonic and I would also like to thank Emily, Elizabeth, Tim, Chris, Al, Sarah, Jenny, Duncan, Caron, Ida and Sally for making me laugh and smile so often. Thanks also to John Featherstone for the cover design and to Clive for your help in editing the book.

I would never have finished this work without the precious love of both my son Alastair and my partner Davina. Alastair, thanks for encouraging me to write books and for all the political chats. Davina, thanks for your patience dealing every day with this grumpy, old soul.

Adrian Warner, May 2019

INTRODUCTION

I knew there was little chance of avoiding redundancy from the British Broadcasting Corporation (BBC) when an important meeting about my future was held in the "Alan Partridge Room" at New Broadcasting House in central London.

Partridge, co-created by British comedian and actor Steve Coogan and satirist Armando Iannucci as a parody of clumsy broadcasting, started his career as a cliché-loving sports journalist before developing into an inept TV and radio presenter in light entertainment. So it was ironic that a huge black-and-white photograph of the English comical character provided the backdrop as an editor and a HR executive went through procedures which led to my 30-year career as a full-time sports journalist being terminated at the age of 51.

It might have been more comforting in a room honouring a great inquisitor and journalist such as Sir Robin Day. Or maybe in one to remember the cool and composed British sports broadcaster Des Lynam? There are many rooms at New Broadcasting House dedicated to BBC legends, both real and fictional. It was a special part of the reconstruction of the headquarters in 2011. But, with all of those great broadcasters to choose from, I was allocated the ludicrous Alan Partridge, adding farce to what he would have called "a bombshell".

It was difficult to take the two rotund middle-managers sitting in front of me seriously with

Partridge shouting his Abba-inspired catchphrase "Aha!" over their shoulders. The farcical mood intensified when halfway through one of the most important meetings of my life, a couple of BBC staff barged in to claim they had booked the room. An argument started to brew with one of the managers about the alleged double booking. It was at that point, that I had the urge to stand up and start shouting.

"Look, I've done a great job here for quite some time --- which you have regularly recognised -- and you are just throwing me away like a finished packet of cigarettes. I don't deserve this. I have a family – a wife, two kids. Don't you realise how much pressure they are going to face? Don't you realise how hard it is to get a job in journalism at the age of 51? Don't you have any conscience?

"Oh and can't you even organise a room in this huge cathedral called Broadcasting House that we can use for an hour without being interrupted? You lot really are just useless and you can go and......."

I wanted to say all of that but, of course, I didn't -- largely because you go through a state of shock when an organisation tells you are no longer needed. The energy you once had for your job in abundance suddenly disappears like a paralysis and you feel numb for a bit.

So I remained terribly English. I smiled at the National Union of Journalists (NUJ) representative beside me, took a quick look at Partridge for comedy inspiration, got none and then asked the interlopers politely to see if they could find another room. Knowing how some of the BBC works, they are probably still looking for one.

In the next year, I would feel a wide range of emotions, from the shock around that meeting to real anger when the BBC insensitively sent me the letter confirming my redundancy 48 hours before Christmas Day when I was hoping for a relaxing family celebration. And then came despair when I went to a Job Centre for the first time to sign on for state benefits.

There was plenty of anxiety and confusion followed by a real fear of how I was going to support my family and pay the bills if I could not find a new job. There was a lot of resentment too towards the people who had done this to me.

Above all, I experienced a huge amount of loneliness, despite the support of people who loved me. Sometimes you feel ignored and forgotten when you need attention the most.

Eventually, hope replaced all of these emotions and the excitement of a new beginning began to sink in. I did change direction and moved on to start another chapter in my career and life. I managed to trust people again and rediscover enthusiasm for another cause. But it was a real roller-coaster of emotions.

If you have been made redundant or forced to leave your job, you will recognise many of these feelings. The reason I have written this book is not to suggest that my redundancy was, in any way, more important than the thousands that are happening every day in a variety of industries and professions everywhere. I have watched many friends and colleagues face the same fate and I have included their experiences in this book too. Redundancy for my generation has become a routine experience, especially for over-50s.

What I have tried to do is put together a handbook to help people deal with the emotions and challenges of a tough time of your life. This book has loads of advice about dealing with the pressures of making a new start and about how to go about changing direction in your career.

I hope it will also help people with the practical techniques of getting a new job which are very different now to what they were a decade or so ago.

Importantly, my aim is to help you (and your partner and friends) understand and handle the painful feelings of loneliness which redundancy can bring -- by being a constant companion during your journey of ups and downs.

I have divided up the chapters into emotions, actions plans and advice about the challenges you are facing. They have simple names, so you can delve into them in the order you wish. You may not need to read every chapter but I hope you find most of them useful. Although my redundancy took place in Great Britain and I do mention some UK organisations, I have tried to make this book very relevant to anybody facing redundancy around the world. I spent a decade living and working outside of the UK as a foreign correspondent for Reuters before joining London's Evening Standard newspaper and the BBC. I speak fluent French and German, so I hope to have an international perspective on life from my 30 years or more as a reporter.

My redundancy in 2014 took place in London where I worked for the BBC as an on-screen Olympics and sports news correspondent but this book deals with issues that will affect you in a similar way, whether you live in New York, San Francisco, Sydney, Wellington, Berlin, Paris or Toronto. It really does not matter much in which industry you work, either. The pain and the pressures are often the same.

There are chapters about 12 key redundancy challenges, from how to deal with anger, managing your money, and relationships with your former colleagues to advice about kick-starting your career, redesigning CVs or resumes and taking a step back to look at your career-life balance in a deep and meaningful way. All of these are relevant to many people, wherever they live on the planet. I have included all of my personal experiences in handling them as well as providing advice. This book is an emotional story as well as a practical guide.

Above all, I hope *Recovering from Redundancy* will make you smile now and again in the middle of the stress of change. This is not a book about 100% positive thinking. I am a 'glass half-empty person' and proud of it. I can't stand all that "being positive all-the-time" stuff. I take the view that it's important to be miserable now and again too, so that you can enjoy it more when things go well.

So I make no apologies for saying how hard it is to walk into a Job Centre and sign on for benefits after you have worked continuously for 30 years. But I hope my experiences can help people handle it, so that they can get back some of the cash they have paid to welfare in taxes over the years.

I make no apologies for saying how it really hurts when you can't even get an interview for a job for which you are perfectly suited. But we will go through that together too, so you can move onto your next role without feeling down about any rejection.

I make no apologies for trying to laugh at the absurdity of life in the 21st century, when CVs or resumes and job application forms are often read by computer programmes before they are studied by people. A wry smile and the odd laugh are crucial for your sanity in the middle of this battle to restart your career.

This book is not just for people facing redundancy but also for their families and friends. It is important for partners, mums and dads or brothers and sisters to understand the emotions people experience when they have been shown the door. I hope my ideas will help everybody to get along better during a time when there is a good chance people are going to grumpy and frustrated on a regular basis.

It is also for managers who make people redundant and want to find better ways of handling the process by understanding how their employees feel. Too many bosses run away from this and take the view that it is easier to force somebody out of the door and to try to forget about them quickly. Too many are happy to run away from conflict but some will almost certainly end up with a bad conscience in the long term. My hope is that this book may persuade managers to behave differently whilst still respecting the orders from the Human Resources (HR) department about legally-sound processes.

I have also written the book for people in a job who are thinking about changing direction in the future. There are loads of tips on how to prepare for a new career or role, so that you are ready to swim straight away, if you are pushed out of the boat without warning. It is often very comforting and positive to feel prepared for change, even if you decide against it or never face it – a sort of career insurance policy. I have kept all the advice short and sharp. That is my journalism training. It should be possible to read each chapter quickly but I have tried to pack in loads of ideas and information. Each chapter starts with 3 challenges ahead in that area and ends with three top tips to remember.

In general, I have written this book so it can be read on the go – on a train or bus ride, during a free moment during a busy day, over a coffee or at a café or pub waiting for a friend to arrive. I want to be a companion who turns up now and again to provide support and advice and then disappears into the background as you get on with your life.

In short, this book is your companion on a difficult but rewarding new journey in your life. Please keep me close on this trip -- maybe even in your pocket or on your mobile device. And I hope we will have a decent chance of making you happy in the future.

I cannot guarantee that everything I have written is relevant to you. You may respond in a different way to your redundancy than I have. I am also not a doctor, therapist or financial advisor and I cannot provide medical answers to depression or anxiety or give you guaranteed financial advice. But what I have put down is a very personal description of what I have learned from my redundancy. It hasn't been easy. One minute I was a BBC correspondent on TV handling a high-profile story such as the London 2012 Olympics and then the next, I was down at a Job

Centre signing on for state benefits because I was struggling to get a job.

I certainly wish I had been better prepared for that day in the Alan Partridge room and the tough journey afterwards. There are so many things I would have done in advance, if I had known it was coming. My goal is to help you learn from my experiences.

Adrian Warner, London, May 2019.

1. ANGER

How to deal with your anger at being made redundant.

Feeling better gradually and making positive decisions.

Taking on the legal questions and being pragmatic about the future.

I left BBC's New Broadcasting House within a couple of minutes of being told I was being made redundant – very much like a footballer storming off the pitch and straight back to the showers after being shown a red card for bad behaviour.

There had been no official warning apart from a blunt text from my boss, saying we had to meet that morning before the department made an announcement. I felt sick when I read it on the train to work, knowing that job cuts were being discussed. I was told to come to a room away from the rest of the newsroom. When I walked in, the two BBC editors did not need to say a word. I knew the moment I saw their faces what was going to happen. They looked embarrassed as they told me my departure had nothing to do with my performance, something which the chief editor later repeated in writing.

The conversation was short and cold. I expressed my disappointment that this had happened after all the good work I had done for the BBC. One of them suggested I took the rest of the day off. "I'm doing that, whether you approve of it or not, " I replied as I picked up my bag and left the room. I haven't exchanged a meaningful word with the editors since, although one did send a card to my home once I had left, thanking me for my work on the Olympics. I am afraid it came straight out of the envelope and into what I call the "round file" – others call it a bin.

I have had a few exchanges with the other editor for operational reasons only. I have no desire to talk to them again for the rest of my life.

Of course, I was angry and I know I will remain angry for years to come. Like anybody being made redundant, I was wounded. You put in great work, your bosses enjoy being associated with your successful stories, and then they just show you the door. It hurts, if you have a sense of fair play in your life. But it is a classic tale and all of us who have been through it feel angry. What matters is how you deal with that anger.

I probably did the right thing in those first few minutes. I did not say a word to any other colleagues and I walked out of the building. The danger with anger is that you often say something which you regret. And you say the wrong thing to the wrong person, just because they are there. None of your colleagues deserves that, so it is best to avoid them.

If you can, I would suggest avoiding them for a few days while your anger is at its peak. If you can get a few days off, take them. Avoid work contacts completely for a few days. You can get the news out soon enough to friends, family and people who work in your field of expertise. We will discuss this in more detail in another chapter.

If you have already been made redundant, the paragraphs above are pretty useless to you because you have already faced this meeting and these emotions. But the anger is unlikely to go away quickly, so it is important to find a way of handling it in both the short and long term.

We all do it -- going over and over things in our minds. It can become an unhealthy habit if you are under stress. So accept that you are going to feel angry and frustrated for quite some time. I am no expert in psychology or mental health (and if you are feeling depressed, always seek out medical advice). But I humbly offer a few tips on how to deal with this.

Firstly, do not try to block these feelings out completely. They are totally normal and, in some ways, mirror parts of bereavement. You are likely to feel numb or in shock for a bit and then you are going to feel anger again.

What matters is that this anger does not get in the way of your future. This will take time. It will not happen overnight and it may take weeks and months before you feel a lot better. So just accept that and start using some techniques to control it on a day-to-day basis.

Some people argue that it is important to find forgiveness and it is astonishing how some victims of crime or wrongdoing can forgive the perpetrator. But is it not for everyone. Personally, I accept that I will be angry with the nature of my redundancy for many years – and possibly for the rest of my life. I have witnessed that view from friends and former colleagues too.

One of the reasons is that I am irritated by the description of the BBC in the UK as some sort of cuddly "auntie". My experience of aunties is that they usually don't look after you for a bit while you are helping them and then suddenly show you the door when you have become less important. There is more long-term loyalty from your average auntie.

So, although I know that there are many decent people working at the BBC at all sorts of levels, my overall experience of the corporation as an employer, is more of a "distant second cousin twice removed" than as an auntie. I am sorry to have to take that view and I am not saying that everybody working there is unloving or uncaring. I am sure the BBC would argue that it is a fair employer which acts within the law -- which it does, of course. I am sure it would also say that it has many happy employees and I met plenty of people at the corporation who effectively worshipped the BBC. Some even still talk about programmes "bringing the nation together on BBC One" like they were some sort of religious awakenings. Whilst I know the BBC is full of journalistic and production talent, I struggle to follow their faith blindly.

But it has a cold commercial side too. I lost my job as part of a series of savings called "Delivering Quality First" when the BBC planned to cut annual costs by £700 million by the end of 2016-17. At the time the BBC said it had benefitted enormously from my role but it was one that it could no longer afford.

Of course, this is a legally sound position but I am allowed to have an opinion on a former employer, too, and the fact is that I may never forgive some of the individuals involved in my departure. You might say that view is too dramatic or emotional and that it is not fair on people who were just meeting demands from their superiors to save money -- following orders. That is a fair argument which I can accept has some validity. The BBC, in that respect, is no different to many companies and managers around the world, who have a close eye on the bottom line and can't afford the luxury of too much loyalty to some employees. The corporation is nothing special, in that respect.

We are all human beings and there was a bigger picture too. I was not just losing a job. My whole career in journalism was put in jeopardy by being thrown out on the street in my fifties when it is much harder to find a job.

You can see I have plenty of anger around my redundancy. What is important, however, is that I have accepted these emotions, locked them away in a "box on the top shelf" (I opened it briefly for this book) and I am not looking to change them.

It is crucial that this sort of anger does not stop you from making your next move. Companies and organisations do not hire people carrying emotional baggage because it gets in the way of their judgement. So it is important to get them into that box on the shelf as soon as you can. This is unlikely to happen in weeks or maybe months. But with every passing day, you will be closer to closing the box and moving on.

Remember, it's hard on your family and friends if you are constantly grumpy. It is not their fault that you have been made redundant and they will understand if you are not feeling great for a while. Understand that they want the best for you and they are probably doing all they can to help. But also understand that sometimes people do say the wrong thing and try not to react badly.

I remember somebody close to me, saying totally the wrong thing when I was criticising the work of a TV reporter shortly after I had been made redundant. Journalists criticise the work of colleagues all the time, especially if they see badly-made TV. But my long-term friend, who was watching the TV with me, said: "At least he's in a job." I don't think that handful of words was supposed to wound me but it certainly did. I felt dreadful.

At first I also found myself spending a lot of days thinking about my experiences at the BBC and getting wound up about my redundancy. It certainly got in the way of thinking up a strategy for my next move. It was also making me grumpy.

So I tried something that a friend of mine once proposed about how to handle worries. If you find yourself going over something in your mind again and again, just say to yourself, "Right I am going to leave that until later in the day, say between 6pm and 7pm.'

So no thinking about the redundancy anger, apart from between 6pm and 7pm. Say that to yourself every day. For a few days, you will think about your frustration for a bit at that particular time, maybe on a walk or while you are doing the dishes and you will avoid it during the rest of the day.

But, quite quickly, you will find that you cannot be bothered because the anger sessions are getting you nowhere. You realise that all you are doing is repeating the same arguments. When you see that, you have broken the cycle of worry.

It is a good technique to use in the middle of night too. If I wake up in the early hours and start going over something in my mind, I always say to myself, 'Right, not in the middle of the night. I will sort this out in daylight." Life seems easier then and you usually fix the problem quickly. I am not a doctor but I do recognise that when you brain is tired, it does not function as well as when it is refreshed.

Of course there will be moments in the future when you feel angry about your redundancy again. That is almost certain. Maybe when you pass your previous place of work or when you come in contact with a former colleague. But those terrible moments will become less frequent.

I was once talking to a friend about his redundancy from a major bank five years previously and it was clear that he was still angry at the way he was treated. This is not surprising since, after more than two decades working for the company, he was asked to pack his things together in 15 minutes and leave the building. The anger was still there in his voice during the conversation but it did not last the whole evening and it certainly was not affecting his everyday life.

For some people, this anger, is like bereavement. You have lost a job, not a person, but the feelings are similar. I have never got over the death of my father

20 years ago but I have learned to live with it. Now and again I feel very sad about losing him but it does not dominate my every thought, like it did in the weeks after his sudden death.

Redundancy anger is similar. It may be that two years after redundancy, you still feel a sense of betrayal at one point in a day. Don't worry about it. The moment will pass.

In those early weeks, just take everything day by day and gradually you will find that you will feel less stress from the actual act of being made redundant. Understand it may never go completely. But, do we ever totally lose those feelings towards people who have betrayed or hurt us? Probably not, but we just try to get on with life.

The reason I have devoted a chapter to anger is that it is crucial that you have it under control and do not let it control you.

Don't take any big career or family decisions in those first few weeks. No decision taken in anger is a good one. Don't go rushing to see future employers in the first week while you are still wounded. Your feelings will show and you are unlikely to impress them. Do not go rushing to lawyers and threatening legal action against your employer or an industrial tribunal straight away. Deal with your anger first and then make those decisions when you are calm.

I rang an employment lawyer a few weeks after my redundancy and got some excellent advice. But only when I was calm and ready to take it in. She told me to take the money and run, even if I felt I had a decent case to take to a tribunal. Would I have accepted that when I was still very angry? I am not sure.

It was good advice. Her view was that a tribunal would not have resulted in a bigger pay-out. So you may get your day in court criticising your employer or bosses in public, but only at the end of months of stress with no money coming in. Why do that? Months of worry for a few minutes of short-lived satisfaction?

I know people who have done this and they really haven't gained from it. And never forget that a future employer may turn away from you, if they are worried that you are too litigious. Is all that morally right? Probably not. Is it hard to take everything on the chin without a chance to have your say? Yes. Will you feel great being kicked hard without a chance to strike a blow? No.

But pragmatism is often more effective than raw emotion in the working world. If you feel you do have a good legal case, then do not hesitate to seek advice from a lawyer. But only after a few weeks or when you can look at the situation with a little less anger. It may be that you have a case for constructive dismissal or for more redundancy money. It may also be that you need to move quickly to get legal advice. If that is the case, try to take anger out of your conversations with the lawyer. It will be hard but you need to weigh up the advantages and disadvantages of what could be a long, legal battle. Revenge is not a good emotion in these cases and it could get in the way of your judgement.

Importantly, do not hesitate to seek medical advice, if you are feel too stressed or depressed. It may be that you need to talk to somebody about your emotions in order to deal with them.

But don't be afraid of being angry. You have every right to have strong feelings about a tough time in your life. But try to control it as the days, weeks and months pass whilst understanding that it may never go away completely. That is fine. You could break your leg and it may not totally recover and you will get the odd twinge now and again.

Most importantly, remember that you can look at yourself in the mirror in the morning and feel that you have acted in an honourable manner throughout, if you keep your emotions under control. That is priceless. People who have made somebody redundant cannot always say that.

Top 3 Tips:

Take your time to get over your anger. It is a marathon, not a sprint.

Don't take any important decisions while you are still emotional about your redundancy.

Understand you may never totally lose all your emotions about your treatment but, with time, you can take decisions with a cool and calm head.

2. HANDLING YOUR FORMER COLLEAGUES

How to understand the different reactions of colleagues to your redundancy.

Drawing up a strategy for relationships with your former workmates.

Saying goodbye and moving on.

It was only when I was clearing my desk a couple of days before my departure from the BBC that I first felt some of the emotion in the newsroom.

Like the most powerful emotional moments, not a word was said. I caught the eye of a colleague who had been watching me throwing away old documents and notes -- putting seven years of reporting and broadcasting into the bin. She was close to tears.

It had been a fascinating seven years of reporting for the BBC as the on-screen Olympics correspondent for the London 2012 Games, covering everything from venue construction to the politics and economics of putting on the biggest sporting show on the planet. I had interviewed prime ministers, government ministers, London mayors and an array of leading sports stars for BBC London, reported from Canada, Greece, China and India for the station and produced plenty of exclusive stories.

I had arrived at the corporation in 2007 after five years in the newspaper world at London's Evening Standard where I won a prestigious UK award from the Sports Journalists' Association (SJA) for my reporting of sports business and political affairs. Before that I had worked for 17 years at the international news agency Reuters, a decade of which was spent as a foreign correspondent living and working abroad.

I have reported from 14 Olympic Games, five football or soccer World Cups and from 25 countries, including nine years as a correspondent in Germany where I witnessed the fall of the Berlin Wall in 1989. But it was in the area of sports politics and business where I had a reputation for getting stories. Sport is a business and the Olympics are much more than three weeks of sporting excellence. The Games provide a 3-week global TV advertisement for a city and a country's image is on the line. At London 2012, there was a lot at stake, economically and politically, and my contacts' book included senior figures in British politics as well as in the international sports world.

Coming to the BBC had been a big shock to the system at first. I had to learn the skills of writing for TV and the presentation techniques of broadcasting live to more than a million people in London. But, with the help of colleagues, I developed into a confident broadcaster. I reckon I did a decent job. I know my work was respected by senior journalists, network editors and by the BBC's Deputy Director-General -- because they all told me so.

In addition to my daily work at the BBC's regional news programme in London, my reporting was broadcast regularly on BBC World, the BBC News Channel and influential programmes such as the TV's 10 O'clock News and Radio 4's Today and PM programmes, BBC Five Live and BBC World Service. I had made documentaries too for the network and after the Games, I took on the role of sports news correspondent for the station.

I mention this, not because I want to blow my own trumpet, but to provide the story behind the simple scene of a middle-aged man packing up his possessions in an office and desperately worrying about his future. Everybody who has done this has an important story to tell about his or her company and career. You don't throw seven years of life away in the bin, of course. We all leave some sort of a legacy behind us in the place where we worked. Sometimes it is new way of doing things that you introduced, or maybe someone important whom you hired. Sometimes it is the guidance you may have given to a younger or less experienced colleague that ends up being your most significant legacy.

That can be remembered for years, just as I still recall the reporting guidance I was given by my first training editor George Short at the international news agency Reuters in the mid-1980s. I still pass on George's writing and reporting tips to my university students today, 30 years on from hearing them for the first time in Fleet Street, then the central hub of British journalism.

So, do not feel that you have not made an impact, just because it is ending – you almost certainly have. In the long term, you will be able to sit back and put some perspective on your career. But in the short term, your challenge is to clear your desk and end your emotional relationship with a workplace and a room full of colleagues.

It was only when my desk was clear and the bin was full of my rubbish, that I really noticed how upset my colleague was. But I said nothing to her and she said nothing to me. Sometimes words are useless – and that from a man who has earned a living from them for decades. We both managed a tiny smile and I left the office with my affairs in a box and my emotions packed away too.

She was a colleague who always had a joke and smile to share every day despite some personal challenges in her life. It had been a joy to work alongside her and her rare sadness that day touched me greatly. To this day, we have never discussed that moment. But I will remember it forever.

I left the kind words to a leaving party which I organised for colleagues a couple of days later – drinks in a pub near the BBC and then a Karaoke session at a bowling alley a short distance away. My colleagues gave me a special framed tapestry with many of the "words of wisdom" I had given them over the years. It was entitled "Warnerisms" and it has a special place in my home.

Importantly, the events were outside the newsroom but close enough that most people would come. I specifically did not want any sort of "corporate send-off" in the office with managers making awkward speeches about the career they had just decided to end. I wanted my colleagues to remember me with a great night of fun, laughter and singing.

I also wanted to take the first psychological step of meeting people away from the place where we had worked together. That was how it was going to be from then on, so I felt it was a good time to lay down a marker. It was a good idea.

Some people, of course, are given a matter of minutes to clear their desk after they are told they are being made redundant, sometimes with a security guard checking their every move in case they plan to sabotage company business in an act of revenge. I have often found that particularly cruel and crass, especially in a world where a business can block somebody from taking action in a matter of seconds - - by simply changing their computer password.

But, whether you are leaving over a period of weeks or just hours, it is important to realise that many colleagues will struggle to know how to react to your imminent departure. A close friend of mine who was made redundant from his company after 20 years, said, of the hundreds of people he knew in the firm, only five made an effort to contact him in the months after he left. I know that he was very popular in the company and the lack of contact hurt him. But it is quite common, so don't be upset if some colleagues find it difficult to express their feelings. Many will avoid you at first because they do not know what to say – not because they do not care. It is important to remember this.

Some, of course, will be glad to see the back of you. The one lesson we all learn in life is that it is impossible to please all the people all of the time. My father, a research engineer and manager in the car industry, used to say that. Not everybody will have liked your methods, humour or even how you dressed. Get over it. But, be under no illusions, that your bosses will probably want you out of the way as soon as possible.

It is hard but try not to take this personally. This says more about them than it says about you.

A journalist I have known for decades once told me about the tough things he had to do as a senior editor. He mentioned having to tell a newsroom that a colleague had been shot dead during an overseas assignment. But he said it was even harder to tell people that they were being made redundant.

It is naïve to think everyone is as sensitive as my journalist friend. But the reality is that your bosses do not want you around because you are a daily reminder of their deeds. They have shown you the door despite all of your good work. They also know that you are a walking example to the rest of their staff that nobody is safe from the axe and that they are prepared to pick it up and use it.

Whenever I had anything to do with my editors in the final weeks of my contract, they often had the look of schoolboys who had been caught red-handed breaking into the tuck shop with a bag full of sweets in their hands. They did not know what to say or, frankly, where to look. It was embarrassing for all of us.

Understand that is often hard for managers to show people the door. They must know that you are going to feel angry about your treatment for a very long time and nobody really likes being disliked. The only exception I have found in this area is a journalist colleague who was once told by her boyfriend-cum-boss that she was being made redundant.

"He told me that he was going to have to make me redundant and then he immediately asked when he could move into my flat," she said. They have since married and have two children. It is the only example of redundancy love I have been able to find.

But she really is an exception and most managers want to keep their distance. So my advice is to stay away from your workplace as much as you can during any notice period. Go to meetings outside, work from home, or just take the day off and plan your next move. Unless you have a job where you have to carry out your duties on the spot and are contractually committed to be there, nobody is going to fire you for not turning up. Remember, they have already decided to end your contract and they can't do it twice. Read your contract, however, and make sure you meet the basic needs of the job in order to get paid.

There is a reason that in some industries, notice periods are usually cut short or people are sent on gardening leave – effectively paid to stay at home and not take up another job with a rival organisation for a few months. The bosses don't like the departing colleague in the office.

But, let's forget them. It is the reaction of fellow colleagues which is sometimes the hardest to take. One friend once told me that he felt like he had a contagious disease when he was made redundant. People avoided talking to him for weeks. They avoided eye contact. I also found that some colleagues were reluctant to talk about my imminent departure. Even those who knew nothing about sport would suddenly take an interest in Chelsea's latest signing in a desperate effort to talk about something "safe".

But that is just human nature and, again, try not to take it personally. Some people struggle to handle people who are seriously ill. They do not know what to say. Other simply cannot deal with issues like friends getting divorced for the same reason. In short, there are people in life who hate dealing with what I call the "dirty nappies of life."

To them, you are a reminder that nobody is safe from redundancy, just as an ill or a divorced person is a reminder that nobody is safe from illness or a marriage break-up. They run away from bad news. That does not mean that they are bad people, however.

Given time, they will contact you or say something meaningful to you when all the dust has settled on your departure. I found messages of support came in conversations months and years later when people explained that they were shocked by what some called the "shoddy" treatment I had received. They were desperate to talk to me and explain.

It is possible that your immediate reaction to this frosty approach is to think that people were only interested in talking to you before because you could help their careers. Now that you can't help them, you no longer matter.

In some cases, this will be true. There will be some who will not want to be seen to be engaging with you because they want to stay sweet with the bosses who fired you. You are damaged goods, no longer the 'in' person. But who wants to know people who think like that, anyway?

Remember that you are hurt, wounded and you will not always think the best of people. In the majority of cases, the dirty nappy scenario is the more likely explanation. With time, you will understand that.

Other colleagues, will, of course, talk to you and try to be supportive. Be grateful for that. Almost all of them will say that you will have no problem finding another job. I heard that so many times. They could not have been more wrong, as I will explain in other chapters. But they mean it sincerely, so take it in that vein.

My advice, though, is to cut your ties with your workplace as soon as you can. It is for your own good. Regular meetings with former colleagues will only remind you of how you enjoyed your previous job. They will not help your recovery. If you broke up with your long-term boyfriend or girlfriend, would you agree to meet her or him or their friends every week afterwards? I doubt it. So don't do the same when your relationships ends with your employer.

Six months down the line – or maybe in a year -- it will be possible to meet up with former colleagues and talk about the old times. But leave it for now.

I kept in touch only with a handful of colleagues whom I would call friends. I would go cycling with one of them, Tom, but I avoided too much chat about the BBC on our 30-mile rides. I used to meet a few others for the odd coffee or drink. But it was not a regular thing – maybe once every few months or so. And I never joined a party of former colleagues unless it was a leaving-do for someone I really liked.

And when you do attend a function, it is important to avoid the occasion turning into a session criticising the bosses. Your friends still have to work for them. Just steer the conversation away from your bitterness towards the organisation. You need to move on from all that. You will always carry some of those feelings but they don't need to be in the forefront of your mind. Those feelings will also not make for a good evening. Bitter is an excellent choice for a beer but a lousy theme for fun.

Seek out your close friends in your industry and your life and focus on them – not on people who were just colleagues. Your friends will want to hear about your progress looking for another job, even if it is not going so well. They will provide advice and new ideas and, if they are really good friends, they will simply listen to your frustrations – and keep buying you drinks. In business, they call it something daft like a blue sky thinking sessions or brainstorming. In real life, it is called having a wonderful friend who listens a lot and tries to make you laugh.

Cherish that. Good friends will let you download your feelings. They understand that you cannot just burden your partner with all your woes and that someone else needs to listen too. One day, your roles are likely to be reversed, given the nature of employment in the 21st century. So don't feel guilty about being the one who is downloading the rubbish this time. One day, you will be listening to their frustrations after redundancy and buying most of the drinks.

You will remember their kindness and their help for the rest of your life. And you will have a special bond for years to come. It is true that you discover your true friends in difficult times. I did.

But, however hard it is, break your ties with your former colleagues. They will understand. Avoid going to your former workplace, unless it is to discuss potential work for another department. Avoid work parties or drinks. You do not work with them anymore. You need to make a clean break.

Top 3 tips:

Remember that many colleagues will struggle to know what to say to you. Give them time.

Put clear water between you and your former workmates. Avoid too many social gatherings.

Seek out true friends and download your emotions, if you can.

3. A FRESH START

Drawing up a creative strategy for a new start.

Making new contacts.

Putting the news out to your industry that you are looking for work and getting advice.

Successful football players don't score goals through luck. Strikers run hard to get into the right place at the right time to slot the ball into the goal. Of course, most people only see the tap-in, so they assume it's easy and it is just about luck. It isn't, by any means.

The common characteristics of the hundreds of successful sports stars I have interviewed over more than three decades are skill, determination, planning and hard work.

Major figure such as footballers David Beckham and Ronaldo, rugby players Jonny Wilkinson and Richie McCaw and Olympic athletes Usain Bolt, Seb Coe and Kelly Holmes all achieved their success through hours of obsessive practice and training.

I have seen the same organisational skills and determination in rock stars. Don't be fooled by the image of musicians just strolling onto stage, like they would waltz into a hotel breakfast room. Behind that relaxed image is usually someone who has an intense attention to detail in rehearsal and has warmed up his or her voice carefully in the dressing room before the gig.

I have been lucky enough to perform live as a backing singer for a number of top pop stars, including Ray Davies of The Kinks and Noel Gallagher, formerly of Oasis. It is part of the singing I do with Crouch End Festival Chorus, one of Britain's leading choirs based in north London.

What I learned in these gigs is that rock stars put a lot of time into their preparations and rehearsals in order to look relaxed when they perform. Ray and Noel have an attention to detail in rehearsal which is easily on a par with the dedication of any top-class sports star.

It is the same for the rest of us. I remember a famous journalist once telling me that he had never been offered a job. He had always had to lobby for a role and nothing had come straight to him because of his reputation. I was surprised because he was very good at what he did and was a pioneer in his area of journalism. I had always assumed that jobs came to him, rather than the other way around.

The fact is that good people make getting a job look easy. But don't believe it is easy for a second.

So the first lesson to learn is: Don't expect the phone to ring non-stop or your email inbox to be full of offers of jobs when people hear you are available. You have to make it ring. You have to send the first emails. Most importantly, you need to draw up a plan of action.

Once you feel happy that your anger is under control and you are ready to be positive about the future – for most of the day, anyway – start thinking about this.

Clarity of thought is important but it is also a major challenge. You may be at a stage of life where you want to do something different. I certainly was. I knew I was not going to get the same kind of full-time role I had enjoyed at the BBC, the Evening Standard and Reuters because the industry wants younger – and cheaper – staff. I had seen other journalists of the same age or at a similar stage of their career leaving the industry because of this.

So I needed to work out exactly what I was going to do. I had thought about university lecturing, about communications and about freelance work but I was far from sure what I wanted next. I was also unsure what was possible. This is a major life decision. It needs time, perspective and creative thinking.

But, the problem is, most of us don't have much time. The redundancy payment – if you get a decent one -- does not last forever and there are bills to pay. So you are probably going to end up trying to work out what you want in the next 10 years at the same time as sorting out your finances for the next few months.

It is a very difficult juggling act, but, don't worry, we are all in the same boat and there are solutions.
If you can give yourself some time, it is an advantage. We will look at money matters in another chapter but I managed to work out a financial plan which meant I could survive for six months without working too much while I looked for a job. I really needed that

time to get my act together, especially since I was looking to change direction.

The danger, of course, is that people jump into the first job on offer out of sheer panic and end up going down the wrong path and feeling unhappy. It is easy to understand how that happens but it is best to avoid a decision taken under duress. So starting trying to think about both the short term and the long term together.

The first thing is to tell the business world where you have worked that you have been made redundant. Whether you are a plumber, banker, journalist, sales executive, your friends and all the people involved in your field need to know.

Do not feel ashamed that you have been made redundant. It is fine to feel anger, as we have analysed earlier, but it is not right to feel embarrassed. You are not a failure.

Decisions to make staff redundant are almost always taken because of cost, not because of poor performance. I had become too expensive for my TV department, together with another senior correspondent (Kurt Barling) and a well-known weather presenter (Peter Cockcroft). All three of us had done our jobs very well, according to management, but all three of us were also over 50 and on decent salaries. We were shown the door because the BBC needed to save money and had to axe staff. Let's face it, in most businesses – from meat factories to second-hand car dealerships – the opinions of the accountants usually rule the day in the end. The BBC is no different.

So, whilst you might feel anger at the injustice of the decision, you should not feel any embarrassment.

It is happening to hundreds of people – if not thousands --- every week. I have always been of the opinion that often organisations are full of too many people who know the price of everything but the value of nothing. It is the bottom line of capitalism.

So get that the news out into your market. That was relatively easy for me. The Sports Journalists' Association (SJA), where I had won an award for my reporting at the Evening Standard, has a website which carries stories about members and they ran a story about my departure from the BBC.

The good thing about getting my news out that way was that I was able to control the message. There was no speculation about why I had gone or any ill-informed gossip. The headline said I had been "axed" which was pretty much true. I wasn't afraid of letting it be known that they had made me "compulsorily redundant" ie that I had had no choice in the matter. I also ran the story on Twitter and Facebook with a link to the SJA story.

The National Union of Journalists (NUJ), the union I first joined when I went to work in Fleet Street in 1986, was unable to stop my compulsory redundancy, although it did provide some legal guidance in the process and helped me to deal with the BBC's HR Department, where I did need moral support. I have since decided to cease my NUJ membership but I do now belong to the university lecturers' union (UCU). I have not given up on unions completely because they do have some collective bargaining power.

Later in the process when you are dealing with new employers, you may decide to be more vague about whose decision it was to bring about the redundancy (simply because it is in the past and doesn't really matter anymore) but, for now, honesty is important. Just make it clear that you have not been made redundant because of poor performance.

Getting the message out can be harder if you work in an industry which does not have websites like the SJA's. Social media is a possible route, such as Facebook or Twitter or another platform such as Linkedin which you know people in your business use regularly. That way, all your friends and contacts understand your position and you do not have to explain the situation again and again.

Understand that, even if you put the news out across social media and on a specialist industry website, there will be plenty of people who will not get the news, simply because they did not have time to read it at the time. For a couple of years after my redundancy, I met people who asked me whether I was still at the BBC.

You may decide the best way to inform people is to send out an email to a large number of people, explaining the situation and giving them a new e-mail address where they can reach you. Make it clear and matter-of-fact. Avoid emotion and accusations or bitterness. Leave the stage with a smile. Show your class.

But, however you get the message out, you have to make sure people know. They cannot help you if they are not aware that you are available for new opportunities.

I was touched by the number of journalists who expressed their anger at my departure on Twitter and who praised my work. I avoided making any comment in a public forum – controlling that anger again. But I really did not need to. Other people spoke candidly for me.

I believe you should never criticise your former employers publically because it worries your future ones. Nobody wants to employ someone who is bitter. And they also worry that you may talk about them in the same way, if you move on again.

Whilst I have expressed a few opinions about the BBC in this book a few years on from my redundancy, I avoided criticising the corporation in the first few years after I left. I also believe I have been restrained, factual and fair in this book with explaining my experiences and feelings I now have for the BBC. Only your close friends should know what you really think. I call this "the airline stewardess/steward approach" – always smiling even when they know the plane has hit turbulence.

Anyway, there are more important things to do than waste time criticising your former employers.

Once my story was published, the first thing I did was go to see a friend from my choir who is an expert in getting people into work following redundancy. Edward invited me for a free consultancy session at his home in Hatfield in Hertfordshire. We sat in his living room drinking tea, eating digestive biscuits and drawing circles on large bits of paper. Very English but very effective.

The first drawing focused on my skills. He made me make a list of all the things I could do: write news stories, broadcast, speak fluent French and German, network, produce and edit TV pictures, write books, present videos etc. This is a good way of analysing your abilities. Include all the skills you use in your private life too. You may run the accountancy books for a local running club or get involved in the marketing or ticket sales of a choir or amateur theatre. All of these activities are skills which you might be able to use to make money.

Edward wrote all the skills across the page and circled them. Then he linked them up with lines into the requirements for different jobs. For me that meant all sorts of journalism, teaching journalism or languages, translation, communications, corporate video work, teaching presentation for executives. He listed all sorts of different roles.

Try this out with a friend or colleague who knows you well. It will make you think laterally about what your next move could be. It is also good for your confidence when you realise you have far more skills than you ever thought. It will also make you aware that you have the skills for other jobs too. I have a friend who used to work at 10, Downing Street for a British Prime Minister and who has since re-trained as a teacher via setting herself up as a manicurist. You will be surprised what you can achieve.

There was a crucial second part to Edward's tea-time consultancy session. He took another large sheet of paper and asked me to list all the people I knew on it, writing their names across all the space. He made me write the names of not just work contacts but friends and people I knew in my private life together with their professions.

Then together we worked on which key figures they actually knew themselves in terms of contacts and what they knew about. Your friends and colleagues may be able to put you in touch with people who would be interested in employing you or could offer advice on another career. This ended up being an important route for me in finding new work. Edward's drawing marked the start of it. I still have it in my study.

If you try this, you will almost certainly need a large piece of paper because you are likely to draw a very busy diagram. But from it, you will be able to get some clarity of thought and see whom you need to contact to start your journey to success.

Some people in business say that around 70% of jobs are not advertised. Read that number again and think about it. You can spend a lot of time looking for jobs on specialised websites for your area or profession but you are only going to get near that 70% if you talk to people and find out about the opportunities coming up. In truth you need to plan to do a mixture of looking for advertised jobs on websites at the same time as trying to find out about the many opportunities which are not advertised. While you are doing this, you can also explore the ideas of using your skills to do a different job. Meeting people is an important part of this.

So take this list and start contacting people. A good place to start is by arranging meetings with people who work in your field whom you have always liked. Do not ask them for a job. That may make them feel pressured and defensive from the start. Just drop them an email or give them a call, and say you would like to meet for some advice. A coffee is always better than a telephone call but, if they are super busy, settle for the call.

I arranged plenty of coffees like this and learned a great deal from them. I arranged meetings with a wide range of people whom I know – from the late Labour Cabinet Minister Tessa Jowell and PR experts Joanna

Manning-Cooper, Mike Lee and Jackie Brock-Doyle to sporting figures such as the former UK Athletics chair Ed Warner and the London Legacy Corporation's Victoria O'Byrne. They all had interesting advice to give. I had other meetings with headhunters and sports editors across the media and I took a lot of personal advice from my friends Kurt Barling, Neil Heydon-Dumbleton and Ian Chadband.

All of these meetings were brainstorming really. What you are also doing is saying 'Look, I am in the market if you hear about a job' or 'I am looking for a change of direction'. Do not use the meetings to complain about your former employer – even if you are asked about why you left. Use them to ask for tips on how to move on. A positive attitude is important at all times.

Always ask at the end if they could recommend someone else to talk to. They may be able to help you meet somebody who is working in exactly the area into which you want to move. Always come away with a new name, a new contact to email or ring. A speculative email with the support of a contact has always got more chance of success than cold calling.

Stagger these meetings. You may be looking for several months for the right job and it is good to have appointments to keep your busy and sane. Make a point of having at least two meetings a week set up, maybe on the same day to save money if you need to travel to the same place.

You may decide you want more meetings at the start to find out about the marketplace. But always keep working on setting them up. Even if you get a temporary job to pay the bills for a few months, keep your schedule of meetings going. I always felt better after a coffee with a contact because I was actively doing something to improve my position. I made sure I came away with new ideas and a new list of people to contact. Ring the people with whom you cannot arrange a meeting but, above all, talk to people and keep your ear to the ground. That is the only way you are going to get close to those 70 % of jobs available and it is the only way you are going to get practical help if you plan to change direction in your career.

When you do this, it is crucial to remember two things:

1. *TIME* - Other people are working on a different time to you. You are desperately trying to improve your situation as quickly as you can whilst the people you are contacting are operating on a slower, routine basis. This is the same time on which you used to operate in work. It's not slow – it's totally normal. The fact is that they have many other things to do and might forget your request for a while. So don't get frustrated if people do not take action straight away. They will get around to helping you in the end. Just remind them about your request after a week or so in a polite way. A week is a long time in job hunting, I know, but try to put yourself in the position of the person helping you and show patience. I found people contacted me sometimes months after a meeting to tell me about openings. I found friends had been thinking about my hunt for a job but they just did not have anything appropriate to send my way immediately. It does no harm to remind people about your inquiry with a second email but don't send one after just a week. Give it a little longer.

2.   *HOPES* - There will be moments when you come away from a meeting feeling very positive about possible opportunities but they lead absolutely nowhere. This is not your fault and it is not the fault of the person you have met either. Sometimes people are too optimistic about being able to help you and then find that their company is not in a position to offer you a job. That is an embarrassing situation and the person you have met might be reluctant to tell you the bad news. Most human beings avoid awkward moments by running away from them. I had quite a few meetings where I had spoken to contacts about freelance work, felt the conversation had gone well but was then faced with deathly silence. Don't over-analyse the situation, take it on the chin and move on. Remember, it is a numbers' game.

Don't rely on one contact too much and make sure you have loads of conversations and emails going on at the same time. You are fishing and only need one of them to lead to securing your future.

Like top sports stars and musicians, make the hard yards and get into the right position to reach your goal. In your case, meetings, emails and calls are replacing training runs and intensive rehearsing sessions. But you will learn so much from them and feel better psychologically because you are actively trying to improve your situation.

Top 3 Tips:

Carry out a thorough analysis of all your skills.

Make the phone ring and the email inbox fill up by contacting people and arranging chats about your future.

Ask people for advice --- not a job -- and come away from every meeting with the name of another person to contact.

4. CVS AND APPLICATIONS

How to create computer-savvy job applications for the 21st century.

Selling yourself concisely with your top three skills.

Tailoring your CV and application for every job.

We live in an era where some people choose prospective lovers with a swipe of a thumb on a phone, where every search on the web can lead to a daily shower of adverts and where computerised voices ring up and offer compensation for insurances schemes you have never taken out.

It is getting to the ridiculous stage where companies advertise the idea of being able to talk to a human being – rather than a computer --- as a real incentive to do business with them, rather than a given.

In my fifties and sometimes a grumpy, old soul, I struggle a bit with all this. My experience is that websites and computerised voices don't understand irony, anger, humour, sarcasm or plain and simple complaining. And I quite like a bit of that in my everyday life. Crucially, computers don't really think creatively or laterally -- yet – and I think that is quite important in life.

However, you and I have to learn to live with the new world of computerised job-hunting in order to survive. So let's get used to it.

It is very possible that the curriculum vitae (CV), resume or job application you send off will not be read first by a human being at all. Many companies now use computer software to scan forms for key words and decide whether you are going to reach the next stage of the process. This is known as an Applicant Tracking System (ATS) and you will need to learn how to beat the "bots".

So it is crucial that you use the key words in the job specifications and advert to have any chance of getting through. If you were called a marketing manager but the job advert talks about a "marketing executive" then use the latter. If the specifications keep mentioning "managerial skills" then make sure you have that term several times in your CV or application form. If the ad talks about a "content provider" instead of a writer, make sure you use that term, whether you like it or not.

Identify the key elements of the job specifications and skills and make sure that you have mentioned them in the statement supporting your application. The computer could well be looking for a number of matches and highlighting them.

It is also important to use a format for any CVs/resumes or documents which is recognised by the company or organisation's software. Look out for suggestions on this in the forms provided. I would also recommend avoiding graphics and charts because there is a good chance that the ATS will not be able to read them properly. These kind of systems are changing all the time so take a few moments to read up on the latest analytics changes on the Internet.

This will probably mean that you will have to re-write your CV each time for every individual job application. I did. I lost count of the number of times I re-wrote my resume, so that it met the requirements of the job specifications. It must have been hundreds of times. I applied for jobs as the editor of blue chip company websites and a national newspaper. I went for communications roles in sports bodies, an embassy (needing a fluent Geman and French speaker) and an international charity. And every time I approached an organization for contract work, I re-wrote my CV to highlight my knowledge in the area of business. I never exaggerated my expertise or turned my CV into fiction. But it needed what we call "a new top" in the journalistic world.

Of course there were times when I grew tired of making the changes, especially when I knew I was probably too old or not experienced enough for the role.

You may not like adding in terms which you personally would not use. But that is tough. It may be a tedious process but it will be crucial to you getting to an interview. You have to get enough points in the scanning process to get to the employer.

Some companies may even use a computer game with scenarios to assess your suitability. Think very carefully about what they want you to say and why they are asking a particular question and answer accordingly. Don't try to be clever or humorous. That might work with people but it certainly does not work with machines.

Is this all a good way of companies finding suitable candidates? Of course, it isn't. Forgive me, blue chip executives, but I think it is totally bonkers. I understand how you are trying to save money and time but excellent candidates with an interesting CV could miss the cut in the first round simply because their application is far too eloquent and has failed to use the words in the job specifications. A human being would spot their talent and potential. Computer software will not. I know a very talented young woman, with an excellent degree, who failed to get past the online question and answer session to work in a high street store.

Not all job applications are analysed by computers. I once rang up a chief executive and he said he was in the middle of going through 60 applications for a communications director role. Given that he would work closely with the successful candidate, it made sense that he had a hands-on approach and he was prepared to do the hard yards.

But many other employers do not have the time to sort through hundreds of applications and they turn to software to help them.

So, don't fight it. Play the game. Highlight the key words and make sure they are in your application. Always fill in every section – even if that means writing N/A – not applicable.

The danger with all this, of course, is that you end up writing an application of business gobbledegook. What happens then, if there is a chief executive at the start of the process who is not impressed by jargon?

That is the risk you have to take because the chances are a computer will be reading your material first of all -- in both large and small companies.

The best solution, in my view, is to provide the key words for the computer together with clear descriptions of what you have done and how that is relevant to the job specifications. It is also important to be aware that the computer software may search for the key words early in the application letter, so do not be afraid to mention them early on.

There are many books on how to write a CV and many websites and theories about which approach to take. I am not going to take you through all the techniques but I will point out a few things which I believe are important. I learned them from my friend Edward, a recruitment expert who has helped many people get a job following redundancy. Here are three key points to remember:

1.   Always begin your CV with a short resume of who you are. For example…

Award-winning journalist with 30 years' experience of reporting for Reuters, Evening Standard and the BBC as a sports correspondent for TV, radio, online, newspapers, agency and social media. Covered 14 Olympics and 5 football World Cups. Freelance writer and broadcaster, media trainer and Senior Lecturer in Multimedia Journalism at the University of Northampton. Fluent French and German. Very experienced in live TV and packaging. Author.

The reality is that a recruiter is unlikely to have the time to read every word of the CV, so don't leave the best bits until the end. Get to the point straight away with the highlights --- and tailor the highlights to the job in hand. Only when you have done that, can you go into the chronological list of your previous roles, detailing what your duties were and what you achieved. The CV should be no longer than two pages of A4.

2.   Re-write your CV every time for every job, especially the start. Slot in the key words from the job advert and tailor your CV to the job specifications. This takes a lot of time but remember, the reader is looking at it for the first time. There is little point in highlighting your TV skills, if the job is editing a magazine. Think about what you would look for, if you were the recruiter. This may be different to what you see as your greatest achievements. So switch your focus to what the recruiter wants and match your skills to those needs, rather than just highlighting all of your skills, some of which may not be relevant at all.

3.   People often forget to highlight their achievements. This is a big mistake. If you have won awards, always mention them in the CV. If you were salesperson of the year, tell your potential employer. If one of your projects won recognition in your industry, get it into your CV. Always tell the truth – you will get caught out exaggerating -- but forget modesty and sell yourself. Nobody else will.

Evidence must be at the heart of your CV. Too many people write a CV full of adjectives and skills – passion for this, knowledge of that, dedication to the cause. On their own, these words do not mean a lot – and everybody else's CV will probably have them. You need to stand out from the crowd by providing evidence of what you have actually done in your various roles.

So, instead of filling your application with these kinds of descriptive words, try to think how you might be able to provide evidence of that knowledge, dedication or passion. Tell the employer that you have 10 years' experience of doing something and detail what you did. That shows dedication and passion. Provide evidence of how you changed things. That shows clear commitment and creativity. In short, don't just use words which everybody will use. Provide the evidence of action which shows that you can live up to those labels.

When you match the job specifications to your statements, always think of an example which provides evidence of your skills. A recruiter wants to know how you solved problems or led teams in the past. This also provides you with examples on which to expand in an interview situation.

Remember, sometimes it is equally as hard for interviewers as it is for candidates to get the conversation going in an interview situation. People often forget that. By providing specific examples where you have used your skills, you are giving the interviewer an easy subject about which to ask you questions.

The most important thing with filling out application forms is that you need time. Don't leave it until the day before the deadline. Get on with it straight away. You may need to attach something.

I learned that applying for jobs is a full-time occupation, much harder than going to work. It is a lot less rewarding too. You can spend hours doing an application and end up getting nowhere. We will talk about rejection later.

But treat every application with the same attention to detail and determination to succeed. Accuracy is important. Check everything you write for grammar and spelling and make sure that you produce the best application you can. Poor grammar and spelling is like a crooked tie or a scruffy outfit. It may not be relevant to the job in hand but it creates the wrong impression.

Above all, remember that this a numbers' game. The more applications you do, the more chance you have of getting an interview. But they have to be good applications. So quality and quantity count.

Always keep a copy of what you have done and file them on your computer. A lot of your applications will contain the same selling points, so you can re-cycle some of your work, even if you have to tailor the CVs or resumes to the job in hand.

Work hard on your cover letter too. This should be short and to-the-point. In essence, it should highlight the three main reasons why you have the experience for the job.

Remember to keep it short but make sure you use the words from the job specifications as well.

Here is a fictional example:

Dear Mr Johnson,
I should like to apply for the role of Head of Website Content at the England and Wales Cricket Board.

I have attached my CV below. You will see it shows:

* Exceptional verbal and written communications skills and detailed knowledge of producing content for digital media after 30 years as an award-winning text and on-screen TV sports correspondent for Reuters, the Evening Standard and BBC, including many hours of live broadcasting and work broadcast on opinion-forming programmes such as The 10 o'clock News, Radio 5 Live, Radio 4's Today.

*Ability to give strategic advice, promote the Board and develop crisis communications through intensive involvement as a regular media consultant and trainer to doctors and senior staff on NHS Leadership Academy programmes, to business executives through the Thomson Reuters Foundation, and to university vice-chancellors.

*Knowledge of cricket through past reporting of the game and through wide experience of covering international sport around the world, especially the politics of the IOC and 14 Olympic Games. Excellent contacts with editors and correspondents across the national and international sports media.

I look forward to talking to you how I could play a positive role in this position at the Board.

Yours sincerely

Adrian Warner

If you need to provide a personal or supporting statement, focus again on the key job specifications and skills. It is useful to break up the statement into headlines eg Sales experience, management skills etc and to put those headings in bold. This makes it easier for an interviewer to read and to focus on the areas which interest them. Sometimes people interviewing candidates do not have a lot of time to read up on every candidate. Make that easy for them.

A well-presented statement also says a lot about a candidate. In the job, you may have to write or present reports and a clear application indicates that you have the skills to do that well. It is much tougher to reduce an idea to 200 words, than it is to write 2000. But 200 words of clear language will often make a bigger impression than a long, rambling presentation of clichés and management speak.

A well-presented list of your qualities also indicates an individual who has clarity of thought, another skill which is important for many jobs.

Don't forget the things you may do as a volunteer in your personal life. If, for example, you run the public relations for your local rugby club for free, that may show you have developed skills in that area – even if you have not been paid for it and do not regard it as part of your professional life.

There are, of course, many different ways of writing a resume or CV and some professions demand another style with far more detail eg the academic world and health service. So this is not meant as a size-fits-all CV. But if you are looking to make your resume easier to read, it is a format which could fit the bill.

I developed a love-hate relationship towards trawling through job sites and filling in applications. I re-wrote my CV at least a hundred times, each time knowing that my application might not get past the first hurdle. In essence you are cooking with the same ingredients every day but somehow trying to make them taste different each time.

I could do this reasonably well. Ironically, I am quite good at looking at what is left in the fridge and turning it into a meal and I have been trained in subbing – which is often about turning somebody else's ordinary reporting into a better written story.

More importantly, I also know that it is a very comforting feeling to send in applications, because you are doing something positive about trying to find a new job.

My father used to say to me: "If you can do something about a situation, do it. If you can't, then don't worry about it. "

It is hard to stop worrying, of course, but it was good advice. You can do something about finding another job, so get down to applying for jobs at the same time as working on your networking.

Top 3 Tips:

Make sure a computer programme can recognise your skills by using the exact terms in the job specifications.

Identify the three main reasons why you are perfect for the job and highlight them in the cover letter.

Don't forget to mention your achievements and awards as well as your qualifications.

5. ARRANGING YOUR DAYS

How to make working from home a success.

How to strike the right balance between job hunting and relaxation.

How to feel healthy and happy and develop a routine to your home working.

When you are in work, you have a reason to get up in the morning, a timetable to follow and the reward that when you do the job properly, you will usually get paid – even if it may need a few reminders to your client.

Some people may not acknowledge it but hunting for a job is a lot harder – and often a lot less rewarding.

You can spend half the day trying to contact people for meetings and reach nobody. You can spend a lot of a week filling in application forms which eventually lead to rejections. None of this is going to lead to a single penny or cent going into your bank account.

Please don't tell me that it is an easy life being unemployed – as some people stupidly claim. I worked continuous for three decades and then I had a year out of work. Being unemployed is, by far, a tougher way of living.

It can be extremely frustrating and distressing dealing with the ups and downs of hunting for a job. I would certainly rather be doing pressured 12-hour days in work than face the more intensive stress of looking for a job.

But it is important to structure your life, so that you can get some satisfaction from your days, even if they are frustrating. Here are my eight top tips for working from home. Many of them also apply to anybody who is working from home for the first time, not just to somebody seeking work.

1.   DRESS FOR WORK

Get out of bed in the morning as if you were going to work. Rush around sorting out the family or the dog -- as you would, if you had to leave your home and go to an office or another workplace. Set yourself a start time to sit down and look through the various websites where you can find possible employment or make phone calls. Make sure you are not late starting this. Some home workers have told me that they dress as though they are going to an office. So they don't lounge around in scruffy clothes, unshaven or unwashed. I am not sure wearing a suit or a work outfit in your study or kitchen is a good idea but at least prepare yourself to be presentable.

You never know, somebody may ring you up and want to meet at short notice. There may be no time to shave or wash your hair before rushing off to a meeting which could turn out to be important. Discipline is important, though. You will feel better if you are dressed properly and ready to go.

2. CREATE A DEDICATED WORK SPACE

Some people are lucky enough to have a study or spare room in their house which they can use as a work station. If you haven't got a study, try to find a place in your home which is separate from the rooms or areas which you use for relaxation, cooking or playing with your children. It may be just a table in the corner of the living room or kitchen but try to keep it as a place that you use only for work. Then you can psychologically switch from the fun places of your home to the work station. You can also leave your books and papers there, so it is easier to return to work when you need to. Some people convert their sheds or their garages into work stations, so be imaginative about this. Make you work space very practical. A printer is useful, if not essential in today's electronic world. Create an electronic and/or paper diary, so you can keep right on top of meetings you have arranged and it is also useful to keep a record of what you have achieved every day.

3. ALWAYS TALK TO SOMEBODY OR E-MAIL A CONTACT EVERY DAY

Send at least one email and/or make a call aimed at setting up a meeting every day. You need to be working regularly on improving your network of contacts. It is important to be talking to people about your future all the time. If you can't reach somebody new, talk to a former colleague or friend about any news they may have about openings. The conversations do not need to be long but keeping in touch with your market is crucial, when you are working from home. A friend or a colleague may have heard something on the grapevine which might be a wonderful opportunity for you. You will need to follow it up. Answer missed calls as soon as you can. On that note, make sure your mobile phone reception at home is good enough. These days, you do not need a phone landline, although it can be helpful, especially, if your local mobile phone service can have problems. I once had to switch mine because I was missing too many work calls. For sanity reasons, it is also crucial to try to talk to somebody every day, especially if you are alone in the house. Otherwise you will end up talking to yourself – never a good thing in the long term because the conversation is very predictable.

4.   TAKE BREAKS

You need to be hunting hard for a job but there is only a specific amount of time you can do this without losing your mind. Set aside time for your website trawls, your calls and emails and any applications you need to make. But take your lunch breaks and find time in the day to go and do something which you enjoy. Go for a run, a bike ride or a walk with the dog during the daylight. Find something that you really enjoy and make sure that you go and do it. This will help you focus on getting your job hunting done in time. Spend more time with your family or partner. When you were working, that was often hard, so use the extra time you have now to make up for that. You will feel more able to do this, if you know that you have put those applications in or made those phone calls to help improve your situation.

5.   KEEP YOURSELF HEALTHY

You are under emotional stress during this time, so make sure you are keeping yourself healthy and fit. Take time to do a healthy food shop for the family and work hard to keep fit. Get outside for some fresh air and keep moving. Don't spend all day in front of your laptop. Keeping a healthy body is good for your mind. Keeping fit will also help you sleep. During times of stress, people often struggle to get off to sleep at night because of their worries. Being physically tired helps this and is a much better solution than alcohol. I used to do a lot of late shifts during my days at Reuters and often struggled to get off to sleep at night when I returned home after midnight. But I soon found that a bike ride home was much more effective than a stiff drink at helping me to relax and get off to sleep. Alcohol may send you off to sleep at first but it is not great for deep and long sleep. Being physically tired from exercise is much better for that.

6.   KEEP A ROUTINE

Work out a routine which works for you. One colleague I know, who works from home, always keeps regular hours and stops working at 5pm. He steps out of his study and shuts the door when he has finished. Then he concentrates on his family and does not answer phone calls or emails outside of working hours. Others find it easier to work a more flexible day. When I worked from home for the Evening Standard, I often used to write from 9am to 3pm in the daytime and then in the evening between 9pm and midnight when my children were in bed. In that way, I could help with the kids' teatime, bath-time and bedtime between 3pm and 9pm and then focus on my work later on. It worked for me because I could check on the next day's papers with the first editions at 10pm and know that I had missed nothing before I went to bed. It also meant that editors would rarely ring me at 5am wanting a story because I largely had my reporting area covered. Another very successful home-worker told me he starts work at 8am but likes a snooze or "power-nap" from 2pm to 3pm. It helps him to function better. If that helps you, do it. I have often found that a quick power nap can be helpful and, if I had a long day broadcasting, I would often grab 30 minutes on a sofa, either near the newsroom, or on location to give me more energy for a live broadcast later on.

7. DON'T BE AFRAID OF DOING EXTRA JOBS AROUND THE HOUSE

You are at home more than ever before. That means you have a great opportunity to do the extra jobs around the house which make life easier for you or your family. This will help your relationship and it will probably save you money. Get the washing on while you are emailing and zap the hoover around, so that you don't spend all day sitting in front of your laptop and keep moving around. This is a great use of time. Think about the time you wasted in an office when you were not really working that hard – gossiping at the water cooler or down in the canteen. Imagine if you could have used those odd 10 minutes to put the washing on or hoover the kitchen. Now you can and it will give you more time to enjoy life with your partner or family. You may also have employed a cleaner before your redundancy but it was one of the luxuries which had to go in your savings. This is an easy way of making up for that without turning your weekends and free time into cleaning sessions.

8. PLAN POSITIVE ACTIVITIES

When you were employed in a job, I doubt that you spent every second of your day on company business. The odd few minutes would have been spent booking a train for a weekend away or a theatre ticket. Don't forget you are allowed to spend time on fun things when you are working from home too.

There is less money around, I know, but try to find something positive to arrange. You will feel better for it. Don't spend all day on it but do take some time to organise the things you love.

Working from home is a challenge, especially if you have never done it before. The big advantage is that you can often get more work done than in an office situation where you can be interrupted by chitchat or colleagues asking advice. The major disadvantage is that you can feel lonely and disconnected from your industry.

So keep in touch with people constantly every day and you will not be forgotten or feel isolated.

Top 3 Tips:

Don't forget to look after yourself in terms of health and relaxation at a tough time.

Make sure you work every day on emailing or phoning people to improve contacts.

Take advantage of the extra time you have for the benefit of your family and friends.

6. MANAGING YOUR MONEY

What to do with any redundancy payment and how to feel happy about it.

Surviving financially without a regular income.

Budgeting for challenging days and how to save money.

I will never forget the day I started to worry intensely about money -- December 15 2014.

It was six months since I had been made redundant and, although I had been working very hard on setting up contracts to work at major sports events for 2015 -including the Rugby World Cup - the cash from my redundancy was running out.

For the first time in my working life, I was seriously worried about how I was going to pay the bills for the first few months of 2015. And I am not talking about going into the red for a few weeks – I mean seriously worried if I could pay them at all. I had used some of my redundancy payment to reduce a lot of debt and had budgeted to live on the rest of the money for around six months.

We were now at the end of this period and, although my wife was bringing home some much-needed income, I had always been the main --- sometimes only -- breadwinner and there was a real worry that we would not be able to cover all the bills starting from January 2015. It was not a particularly comfortable and festive Christmas and New Year.

I had never earned a huge amount of money, so balancing the books was always a challenge every month. But I was lucky that, until now, I had never been kept awake at night, worrying that I would not be able to pay the bills at all.

It was a depressing experience. I had been lucky in my life that I had always been in work throughout most of my 20s and all of my 30s and 40s. Many are not so lucky and have faced this situation more times than me. Nevertheless, it was stark exposure to the perils of the modern life.

All we ask for in our lives is to be able to put food on the table for our families and to pay for the roof over our heads. When there is not enough money coming in to do that, you feel sick to the bottom of your stomach.

My search for a permanent job had been fruitless. Application after application. Phone call after phone call. Meeting after meeting. It had all led to nothing. I knew there was work on the horizon later in the year and I had set up contracts at major sports events from the middle of the year. But there were six months until then -- half a year of bills to be paid and a family to be looked after.

As I write this chapter four years on, I have just received a telephone call from the man who came to my rescue. Ironically, he is ringing for advice about freelance work. The boot is on the other foot and I spent an hour giving him help – as much as I could. What he doesn't realise is that he got me out of a big hole at the start of 2015 and I owe him a lot. I had heard from a friend that he needed journalists to help rewrite the website of a major London university where he was working in public relations. It involved interviewing academics and re-writing the details of the postgraduate courses in a major redesign of the university's website.

There were loads of courses to write about and a friend of mine told me that they needed extra people. I jumped at it and for two months, I sat at my desk at home and wrote about everything from criminology and sociology to politics and international development. It was very different work to the sports and news reporting I had carried out for three decades. But it was using the skills I had to make money. Was it what I wanted to do for the rest of my life? No. But the daily fee paid the bills and I managed to get through that difficult period, after which I was able to secure my first job as a university lecturer and earn a regular income.

Whilst it is crucial to start thinking long term about the rest of your life, there are moments when pragmatism must rule your days and financial planning.

This is the most difficult balancing act in the first year after redundancy. You want to think about the long term and how you are going to change direction in life. These are big decisions to make but, at the same time, you need to make sure you can pay next month's gas and electricity bills.

Most people in most countries get some sort of severance payment for their redundancy. Sometimes companies pay the bare minimum for the number of years worked, which is about a week and half's pay for every year in the UK, if you are over 41. It is less, if you are younger. Others pay around a month's salary per year worked, £30,000 of which is not taxed in Britain. Each country has different systems and it is best to check government websites to see what are the statutory payments for continued service. Australia seems to have a similar system close to the UK's, although employees at the start of the scale get four weeks for a year's service.

In the United States, there appears to be no legal guarantee of severance payments at all and it just up to agreements between employers and employees. So check what your rights are by law and make sure your employer is offering you the money it must by law.

Of course, there are people who receive huge bonuses of hundreds of thousands of pounds or dollars when they leave a company. Sometimes these deals involve "gagging orders" or confidentiality clauses which stop the employee talking publically about their departure or the company in return for extra cash. But these kind of deals are usually in the minority. Most of us are not dealing with such large sums. But, whatever your income or severance payment, the principles of managing your budget are largely the same, even if the scale of the payment is different.

I got a reasonable amount of money – more than the legal minimum -- and decided to reduce my mortgage, the loan on my house. I was determined to get something positive out of a negative situation. I wanted to look back at my redundancy and say, "well, at least I dealt with the mortgage a bit and the debt for the house is a lot lower".

Having something positive to say about sad days is a good thing. Use some of the money to take a great holiday to the other side of the world – or use it to start the business you always wanted to. But try to do something which creates some happiness from what is usually a sad moment in your career.

I also kept some cash back in order to live for the next six months. I calculated that it might take a while to get a new job and I needed time – and space -- to get my head around my future. In the end, I needed a lot more than six months to get back on my feet – a year, in fact.

We all deal with money in different ways. Some people look at their bank accounts every day, watch their spending on an hourly basis and are constantly looking for better deals with insurances etc. Other people muddle through life, check there is enough money at the end of the month and just make sure they are okay to pay the mortgage and save for a bit of a holiday.

I belong to the second group. I don't have enough money to make it rule my life and the thought of watching every penny all the time is dreadfully tedious. For decades, I just about got by – paying the mortgage and bills and finding cash for clothes, food and fun for the kids. Most months there was usually a few quid left over for the odd beer, evening out and trip to a rugby or football match, concert and theatre.

But after my redundancy I had to learn to be a lot more forensic with my finances. I needed to be more disciplined with my spending in the short term in order to survive. Do not hesitate to get financial advice, if you think you need it. Some professional advisers I have used did not charge for the first appointment. But, like the help you can get from accountants, good financial advice can save you money in the medium to long term, so it is worth thinking about it. Ask friends for tips on this. Facebook can be brilliant for recommendations. I didn't take any financial advice but I did take some financial action.

It is important to remember that often you can live on a lot less than your monthly take-home pay, if that usually just about covers everything. The six-month figure I calculated for survival, for example, was quite a lot less than my take-home pay for six months.

This is where you need to sit down for a few hours and analyse your spending. A good way of doing this is to go in detail through your bank account for the past few months. See how much money you are spending on everything and write it in separate lists eg food, cash, drinks, bills for your home, entertainment, clothes etc.

In general, this is the best way of getting to grips with spending, whether you are out of a job or not. Some people take a notepad with them for a month and write down everything they buy. This is a useful way of keeping an eye on exactly what you are spending your cash on. This is slightly easier now, if you pay with a card regularly, because you can often see straight away on your account where you have spent your money.

An analysis like this will give you an idea where you can save money. You might be surprised how much money you spend on daily coffee per month – or maybe on those post-work drinks. It might be enough over a year to help pay for an enjoyable weekend away. I had a colleague who would fund his holiday every year by saving money on his lunch every day. He also rarely bought a round of drinks in the bar – not something I would recommend for winning friends and influencing people.

Look how much it is costing you to buy a sandwich every day from your favourite shop. If you need to save this money, change your habits. Take coffee and sandwiches from home to work. Cut back on the drinks after work etc.

When you have lost your job, there is, obviously, quite a lot of money to be saved. I knew, for example, that I would be able to save hundreds of pounds a month because I would no longer be getting on a train to London every day to the BBC. I would need to travel to London to meet people in my job-hunting but I always made sure I arranged meetings after 10am because I could go on cheaper off-peak trains. In addition to providing state benefits, the job centre helped me with a special railcard to go half price too on public transport (please see the job centre chapter).

Those post-work drinks and sandwiches from a central London coffee shop were no longer in my spending either. I trailed through my bank account looking for savings. I am afraid quite a few charity donations had to be cancelled, although I did manage to keep some – there are millions of people worse off than you on the planet, however depressing your current situation is. I also looked for better deals on insurance and energy bills and cut back on TV subscriptions.

This forensic analysis of spending is crucial to getting you through the first few months, so be ruthless with your budget cuts. Of course, you will need to go for the odd drink with friends. It is part of your sanity. But eating out regularly is costly. Do you really need it? Work out how you can save money? Try to live on a lot less money, so that you have more time to sort your life out.

I am not a financial expert and there are plenty of other books, websites and blogs/vlogs about how to run your finances. I once went on a course with a financial expert who explained how she had got into thousands of pounds in debt and needed to cut back on her spending in order to pay back the money.

She recommended always buying the third round of drinks with friends because it was cheaper than the first two. The logic was that the people who were driving would be well into the soft drinks by the third round and others might have to leave after a couple of drinks. It sounds ruthless and I have never been brave enough to try it but she was so determined to save money that she had to resort to it.

On other nights, she said she told friends that she could not afford to go out and couldn't pay her round. Of course, they bailed her out – all good friends would – so in the end she had fun and saved money.

But the most interesting aspect of her presentation was about building up savings. Her view was that anybody in work should always try to save at least six months' living money to which they can get access immediately. As I mention above, this is not six months' salary but the amount of money you could live on for six months, if you suddenly had to give up your job for any reason. It probably equates to about three to four months' actual salary.

This is tough for many people but it is worth trying to build up the cash over a period of time, so that you have the comfort of knowing a financial cushion is there, should your boss show you the door tomorrow.

This is all a bit late for those of us who have been made redundant already, of course. We just have to muddle through and cut back on spending. The key to success here is not to panic. Be forensic and go through your spending in detail. There is always a way of saving money. There is comfort in having complete control over your spending. You will need to talk about all of this with your partner and family and work on it together.

I was fortunate that my children both went to state schools and that I had saved a bit of money towards their university education. There was no need to take them out of private school because we couldn't pay the fees and the impact on their lives was therefore limited. I know this is not always the case for many people and children often face hardship when their parents are made unemployed – whatever the scale of earnings involved. My children still had to watch their spending, however, and that is a good lesson for any teenager as they head towards days when they will be more independent. I made sure that they did not miss out on important trips and school occasions but I told them that money was going to be a bit tight. Both of them showed immense maturity with this. I had   underestimated their ability to handle it all and I was wrong – they were amazing children.

My son told me later that my redundancy had had quite an effect on him. It had sparked his interest in politics and his belief in social justice. I worried about this when he first told me but I was also touched by his compassion. My daughter told me she was very proud of me when I had managed to get another job. I will never forget her words on that important day.

I too was affected by my father's redundancy from the car industry in Coventry in the English Midlands in the early 1980s. He had worked for a company for more than 25 years as an engineer (and was given a gold watch for it) and found himself out of a job at the age of 58. It was tough finding a job in manufacturing in the Midlands, even if you had loads of managerial experience, like he did. It was a boom time for the financial world of London and the south of England but rough for people who lived in the more industrial Midlands and the north of England as well as in Scotland and Wales.

My Dad never worked in the car industry again and I was in my first year at university at the time and was upset by it. When I think deeply about the experience, I realise that it also gave me a strong belief in social justice and helping people in society too. Watching redundancy reminds you about how fragile we all are in our working lives. So I understood what my son meant. Funny how history repeats itself in families.

My Dad made sure the family got through everything okay. That is your goal too. Get to grips with the details of the finances. This will make your loved ones feel more comfortable too. Don't let the money run away with itself and end up in debt. Take financial advice. Maybe it would be better to re-mortgage the house or cut back on every aspect of your spending. It is time to tighten the belt -- probably not for ever but make sure you don't end up overspending.

Shop around for bargains. I discovered that a local supermarket often reduced the price of bread and perishables on Wednesday to ridiculously cheap amounts. You could shop on Wednesdays and pick up some bargains, stick some bread in the freezer and reduce the weekly food bill.

When you are not in a full-time job, you have the time to save cash like this. Use it. It isn't fun, I agree, but it is necessary to get through this period. With a bit of luck, the good times will return.

Top 3 tips:

Do something positive and constructive with any redundancy payment.

Be forensic about your finances and make a big effort to reduce all of your spending.

Take financial advice and avoid building up debt.

7. GOING TO THE JOB CENTRE

How to cope emotionally with going to a Job Centre for benefits.

Taking advantage of opportunities to learn new skills.

Seeking advice from small business experts and Job Centre staff.

I climbed nervously onto my push bike and started cycling across the fields in trepidation. For many years, the rural footpaths at the back of my house had always been associated with fun and laughter and it had been a joy to head off across the fields when my children were young and enjoy an afternoon in the sun together. Now, on this beautiful summer's day, they led to something which I had been dreading for weeks.

It was the day I had to report to my nearest Job Centre in a town four miles away. Since I had left university in the mid-1980s, I had been in uninterrupted employment and could support myself and my family without help from anybody else. For the first time for three decades, I now needed to ask the government to help pay my bills.

It was a demoralising moment, one of the worst of my adult life. Because I had some savings, I was only able to claim the minimum amount in welfare. But it was enough to pay for a week's food shopping and I needed that now.

It had helped that in the previous week, I had, by chance, received a letter from the UK tax authorities detailing how much I had paid in tax in the previous year and what that money had been used for by the government. I could see exactly how much I had paid into welfare, which usually receives a large slice of tax income.

So, as I cycled down the bumpy paths, I kept telling myself that all I was doing was getting some of that money back. The thought helped to lift my mood a little but I was still desperately low. All sorts of questions raced through my mind: What if I didn't ever get another job? What if I couldn't pay all the bills? What if I had to go to the Job Centre for months and months – or even years?

For the first time for weeks, I thought about the people at the BBC who had put me in this position. They had not been in my thoughts as I came to the end of my notice period in the previous months.

But now I was getting angry about them on this bike ride. I had been good at my job but they had forced me out the door, leaving me to seek government handouts. I could sense the warmth of the sun on my back but I felt a cold shiver inside. My anger towards the bosses at the BBC came close to intense resentment.

Many people face this journey every week or fortnight. In my job at the BBC, I had interviewed desperate people outside of Job Centres in east

London, full of frustration that they could not get work. Once, a middle-aged woman broke down in tears as she told me her story in Hackney. Her emotions were so powerful that, after asking her permission, I broadcast pictures of her crying on the news. Before, I thought I understood a bit about unemployment. But in truth I didn't. Only when I went on the dole myself, did I really understand how it felt to be unemployed.

I caught sight of the Job Centre sign as I cycled into the town centre. I hadn't been into one since 1985 when I could claim housing benefit as a student in Edinburgh. Then, going down the dole was a pretty rough experience. We stood in long queues while people argued about their benefits with grumpy staff, shielded from the punters by glass panels. The staff did not seem to like students then. Actually they did not seem to like anyone much and moral seemed low across the board.

So, as I locked my bike up against the railing outside the Job Centre and walked through the door, a feeling of increasing nausea and nerves engulfed me. As a journalist, I had interviewed prime ministers, broadcast live on TV to audiences of more than a million people and faced the pressure of writing important front-page stories for newspapers in 10 minutes. But none of that compared to that moment, in terms of nerves and a feeling of dread and desperation.

I am writing about this candidly because it might be how you have felt or will feel when you think about claiming benefits and have to sign on for them at a Job Centre. These are normal emotions, so try to understand that you need to overcome them in order to receive the payments that you deserve. What is important is that once I had walked through the door of the building, things gradually started to get better.

Firstly, Job Centres in Britain have changed radically since the 1980s. I am sure this is also the case across the world. At many, you have an appointment time, so the days of long queues listening to arguments from other claimants are largely over. Secondly, the staff I met were helpful and showed me respect. They do not hide behind glass panels anymore. At my centre, they sat at desks like any office worker.

The only difference from the average office was that the door was manned by security guards who kept a close eye on people coming in and out and were ready to take action if people did not behave appropriately. These guards also showed respect, just checking my name against a list of appointments and telling me where I needed to go for my meeting. I don't usually need to be called Mr Warner – Adrian will do -- but, for some reason, when I was out of a job, it helped my morale and mood a bit. In short, nobody talked down to me in the Job Centre or made me feel inferior because I was unemployed. We all need respect, especially at low moments.

If you feel uneasy about going to a Job Centre, it is important to keep one thought in your mind: You have probably paid thousands – if not tens of thousands – of pounds or dollars to the government over the years which has been distributed to welfare and you deserve to get some money back at this tough time.

Britain's unemployment benefits are not as good as France, for example, where claimants can get a much larger percentage of their previous salary when they are looking for a job. As I am writing this book, there are huge problems with the new universal credit system of welfare being introduced in the UK. But it is important for you to look into what you can claim back by checking your rights on government websites, wherever you live. In Australia, the benefits are called Newstart Allowance, and in New Zealand, as in Britain, unemployment benefit claimants need to show they are looking for a job. In the United States, unemployment help is usually run by states, so details may vary across the country.

Welfare provision is constantly changing everywhere, so there is little point in going through the pros and cons of current benefit systems in this book because there is a good chance it will soon be reformed again where you live. But go to the authorities and make sure you get the money you are owed.

For me, it meant a fortnightly trip to sign on – the term for putting your signature on a form and showing that you are around in a city or town looking for work. Of course, I didn't like asking for handouts. But as the weeks went on, the bike ride to the Job Centre got easier. More importantly, an advisor there helped me to make the most of my situation.

Caroline (not her real name) did not attempt to lecture me on how to look for a new job. She could see I was looking hard and just advised me to fill in evidence of that on my personal account on the official website – a key part of showing that you are actively looking for work.

Secondly, she found ways to make my job-hunting easier, showing me how to get a railcard for job seekers which made my journeys to London to meet contacts much cheaper. She also took me though the paperwork of claiming for extra money to help support my plans to set up my own freelance company. Although I had read the UK government website in detail before I went to the centre, I was not aware of either the railcard or the extra financial help for setting up a company. So this was crucial advice.

All of this would not have been possible, if I had not walked through the Job Centre door. If you need help to put together a curriculum vitae (CV) or resume and/or advice on writing application letters, the advisors can take you through it or arrange for special courses for you.

Advice on setting up your own business is outsourced to private companies in the UK and I went to see a man who was so stressed with the number of cases he had been allocated, that I immediately felt better about my plight compared to his! I do not think that was the point of the process but his guidance was certainly helpful in the end.

In Britain, many people set up as "sole traders" when they have been made redundant and work for several employers on a fee basis or daily rate. If you want to do this, you will need to get your head around the financial organisation of this. The more you know about issues such as Value Added Tax (VAT), the British tax on business transactions, or filling in tax returns, the better. It can look complicated at first, especially if you are used to just being paid every month and tax being taken off your salary straight away. But a bit of reading of government websites and some accountancy advice will get you back on track. If you can afford it, it is certainly worth employing an accountant who should be able to save you money on tax relief and make sure you are meeting all your tax commitments.

I used to be able claim tax relief in Germany on running a study at home, as long as the room did not have a bed in it, and on the number of days I spent outside of the country working on assignment. In Britain, you can claim relief on the upkeep of your push bike, if it is used to get from your base to a client. So you never know what you can claim as tax relief. All of these small details are meat and drink to an accountant and well worth the fee you will pay to him or her.

If your company offers any free redundancy courses, grab them with both hands. The BBC did give me the choice of doing day courses on organisational matters such as operating as a freelance and keeping finances in check. I joined a handful of people from departments across the corporation in learning how to pressure companies to pay your invoices and how to network and tout for business. They were run by experts and were very useful. Knowledge is crucial here, so if your company offers help, take it – even if the last thing you want to do is go to the firm's HQ. Interestingly, the courses I did encouraged all participants to claim welfare.

Job Centres in the UK, as in most developed countries, also offer claimants the opportunity to do similar courses and advice is usually available in most countries. So swallow your pride, claim the benefit you are owed and look for any extra help which is useful to your future.

However problematic the welfare system is in your country, go and get your fair share of benefits as you prepare to return to the working world. There were times when I thought that, after 30 years of paying into a system, I deserved more than just a minimum payment for six months. I do not believe the British system really gives people enough time to find a job after they have been employed for decades. I used to think that I could always go and earn money in a supermarket staking shelves. But I soon learned when I was unemployed that the local supermarket was very unlikely to employ me because managers would have seen me as overqualified and unlikely to stay very long. Caroline made that quite clear in our conversations. It was a sobering moment since we all like to have a worst case scenario. So the reality is that often people need a lot longer to find the right job than the state allows.

My bike ride did get easier as the weeks went on, however, and I started to feel better about my visits to the Job Centre. Of course, I was relieved when I was able to leave the days of turning up there every fortnight behind me after I found a new job. But the people there did help me in a respectful way and for that, I am very grateful.

Top 3 tips:

Claim your benefits. You have probably paid thousands into the welfare system and deserve something in return.

Get as much advice from the Job Centre on other financial support eg special rail cards and business start-up funds.

Sign up for any useful courses or workshops that are available to job seekers. Knowledge is power.

8. THE BIGGER PICTURE

The importance of trying to think long term as well as short term.

Taking a moment to analyse what is really important to you – career versus personal life.

Taking yourself out of your comfort zone.

One of the best pieces of advice I received in the first few weeks after my redundancy was delivered calmly in a pub near Parliament in Westminster by an old school friend whom I had not seen for years.

"Don't rush into anything," she said. "Think very carefully about what you want to do with the rest of your life. Don't jump at the first thing that comes your way. It has to be right."

Sometimes distance from somebody gives you a better perspective on his or her life. Here was an old friend who had disappeared from my life decades before and lived and worked all around the world. Now based in France, she explained how a close friend of hers had rushed too early into another job after being made redundant and had ended up regretting it a lot.

We were also both in our fifties -- a time of life when people tend to ponder over decisions with a lot more intensity than they did in their busy 30s and 40s when there are often children to be brought up and there is rarely a moment to think beyond plans for the next school holidays.

My options were definitely limited because of my age, especially in a trade like journalism which is more focused on young people than ever before. A business, which used to value experience and standing, seems obsessed with employing young people who, editors believe, are more up-to-date with the latest social media trends. Sports editors are getting younger and younger. So are correspondents as over-50s are shown the door ---- usually before they are ready. The fact is that young people are much cheaper, too. The digital journalism industry is not making anywhere near the money it used to make from advertising in newspapers and editorial budgets are therefore smaller. Knowing that, there was a serious danger I would jump at the first job opportunity to arise because of the worry of not ever getting decent work again.

"Be very careful with that," my friend said. "I know somebody who did that and took a job which really was the wrong thing to do. He got locked in a place where he didn't really want to be. He never really got the perspective he needed on his life."

The problem, of course, is that everybody has to pay the bills in the short and medium term and it is hard to ignore a quick-fix job which solves your financial problems whilst pondering on the rest of your life. It feels like a luxury which you can't afford.

My advice, however, is to think very carefully before jumping at the first job. You need time to think carefully about what you really want to do. You need to answer some questions: Do you want to change direction? Would studying or training for something completely different be better than just taking the same kind of job? Are you actually happy doing what you have been doing for years?

Once you have answered these basic questions, then you are in a better position to plan the future. It may take a few weeks or months to get everything straight in your head.

The problem with switching straight away to another job is that you will not have time to think about these things properly and get some perspective on your position.

Everybody is different, of course, and you might find it easier to take away your financial worries with another job and then be in a position to think about the future. But taking advice from friends, colleagues and experts is hard when you are slaving away at a new job with different colleagues and computers systems. If it is financially viable (we discuss all this in another chapter), it might be better to just take your foot off the pedal and think calmly about what's next.

I really needed the time to do that. I had enjoyed my life writing and broadcasting about sport and I was angry that my career had been brought to an abrupt halt by the BBC at a difficult time of my life. But my conversations with both newspaper editors from Fleet St and with other figures in the BBC had made it clear to me that it was going to be very hard to carry on doing the same job. I think I was too old in the eyes of the new generation of editors, which is hard to take at 51. But I was also probably too expensive as well. In a matter of 5 years I had gone from a reporter who had been offered two very senior roles at national newspapers (and turned them down) to a journalist whom nobody wanted. I know plenty of colleagues of the same age who feel the same about themselves.

It also became clear that it would be very hard to make a living only as a freelance journalist. The reality is that the money is not good enough. I glanced over at a fellow colleague from The Times who had tried to carry on in journalism following her redundancy. She managed to secure a column in another national newspaper. But it clearly wasn't enough and she ended up changing direction completely and has now made a successful career in headhunting executives. Hats off to her. That was a big change and she has completed it with amazing professionalism. It was becoming clear to me that my time in fulltime journalism was coming to an end. It wasn't my choice but I had to be realistic.

So I needed to think about what else I could do – and, more importantly -- what else I really wanted to do. I had been doing some university lecturing whilst I was at the BBC and teaching was an area I had considered developing. I had also thought about trying to get into public relations and working for sporting organisations or event organisers.

I would eventually end up doing a bit of most of this but in the months after redundancy, I needed the time to step back and think carefully about the short, media and long term.

Did I really want to start again completely in a new area of work? That would be going back to square one but I would have to do that to be competitive in the communications world. Was I really capable of changing direction? What were my main priorities for the next few years? Was I prepared to move to another place – to another country perhaps? With fluent French and Germany, I certainly had the languages to do that. I had lived and worked outside of the UK for 10 years of my career. How important was work to me in the next 10 years? Was my private life more important? What about my family, my friends and my activities? Did I really want to give them up and move to another place? Or did I value my family and friendships more than any job?

When you are 22-30, it can be much easier to put your job ahead of the rest of your life. Then children can come along and you have to make career decisions which fit in with your family life in your 40s. In your 50s, your children may be grown up and are already at university or in work and they may not be affected so much by your job. So often, your perspectives and options change with age.

I pondered over all of these questions like you will need to think about the important things in your life. I came to the conclusion that I wanted to be close to my children. I turned down two opportunities which would have involved moving to another country. The jobs were very interesting and exciting. But the reality was that I would not have been happy being far away from my children at such an important part of their lives, even if the job had been fantastic.

I also had friends and activities which were very important to my wellbeing. I spent a lot of time singing in a London choir and I had the chance to perform and record with leading classical and pop music artists and sing in exciting projects. Yes, I could have walked away from them all and attempted to start again in another place. But I was not convinced that this would have made me happy at this stage of my life because I would miss many friends.

When I was in my 20s, I did not think twice about moving abroad to work as a foreign correspondent and, in fact, I lived in mainland Europe for nearly a decade. But this was a different time of my life and I was not convinced I wanted to give up everything – and everybody – that I loved for a job anymore – even if that meant less money and less prestige.

These were my own personal decisions. I was giving up on ambition in return for a happier life. You may have different priorities and that is absolutely fine. Nobody has the right to judge others on this. But what matters is that you are clear in your mind what you really want in the next stage of your life and what your priorities are. The status of a job title is useless, if you are unhappy with your everyday life.

Some people faced with redundancy decide to use some of the money to go travelling. That is another option. Maybe you missed out on exciting holidays at the start of your career because of other priorities and you have a wanderlust now. Why not take that holiday that you always wanted? At least then you can look back at the redundancy period as a positive one because you got something positive out of it. We are only here once.

Or maybe you have always wanted to study for some sort of degree or second degree. This is the time to take the plunge and return to university or college. Work out a financial plan for this and go and talk to universities about how you can make it happen. Sometimes there are special bursaries for people from a certain region or profession. These days it is possible to study over a longer time or even study "at a distance" (ie all the work is carried out online with computer links with tutors and lecturers). Do your homework and try to make it happen.

I had a colleague who wanted to re-train completely as a paramedic. She gave up her office job and carried out all the training for the role. I have plenty of colleagues from journalism who signed up for extra studies in public relations and communications, so that they were in a position to apply for jobs in PR with qualifications.

Eventually I was able to study for a Masters-level Certificate in Teaching in Higher Education (PGCTHE) to become a fellow of the Higher Education Academy. This is an important qualification for teaching and it makes applying for university lectureships much easier since some universities see it as a mandatory criterion.

It was the first time I had studied in a serious way since I took my Bachelor of Arts Degree in French and German Interpreting and Translation at Heriot-Watt University in Edinburgh in 1986. This time I was working as a lecturer at the same time as being a student and juggling my time to fit in all the assessments and workshops with my own teaching. But I soon got into the swing of things and passed the course.

For some people, getting outside of their comfort zone can be as refreshing as getting on a plane and flying to the other side of the world. You will feel better for it – more confident in what you are capable of doing.

Then you will look back at your redundancy and regard it as a time when you changed your life for the better. Rather than being a negative – losing your job – it will become a positive – changing your life for the better through a holiday, studying or a new start.

Take a bit of time to think about what you want…and when you have decided, go for it.

☐

Top 3 Tips:

Don't rush into any decisions. Think carefully about what you really want to do with your life.

Jumping at the first job may not be the right solution. Put long-term happiness ahead of short-term gain.

Think carefully about how your future job will fit in with your personal or family life.

9. REJECTING REJECTION

Handling a ruthless job market

How to deal with rejection letters

Finding a good way of analysing a failed application.

It is a paradox that in an era when it takes seconds to send a message for free from a phone to the other side of the world that many employers do not bother to reply to job applications.

In the months after my redundancy, I spent many hours putting together CVs or filling in application forms for jobs -- drawing up lists of qualities and experience to meet the job specifications, rewriting my CV to match the candidate requirements. Selling myself again and again and again.

But, in many cases, it was all for nothing. Not even a rejection letter. Silence was the response. Indifference to my efforts. The fact is I was simply being ignored. My abilities counted for nothing, so I counted for nothing.

Tens of thousands of people -- probably hundreds of thousands -- face this awful feeling of being ignored every day as they try to get a job. As a journalist, you hope that people are reading or listening to your work. Being ignored is the journalistic definition of complete failure. Psychologically, it is one of the worst feelings on earth. Did it hurt? Of course, it did.

Thirty years ago, I had left a job hunting market where companies bothered to send you a rejection letter, thanking you for your interest in their organisation. When I was at university, I once wrote to every newspaper in the country --- hundreds of letters --- asking for work experience and I received many replies from editors offering me advice and opportunities.

Now, despite the fact that it costs nothing to send an email (and many can be automated), employers do not show the same respect to applicants and often do not reply to applications. I experienced major blue chip companies as well as smaller organisations doing this.

Clearly, there is little respect around for people hunting for work. So there is a massive lesson to learn here: Don't take it personally, if it shocks you. Just learn to live with it.

In Britain we like to think that we are somehow more polite and do things better than the rest of the world. We value a queue, a door opened for manners' sake and we sometimes look down on our European neighbours who are happy to form a scrum to get on a bus or buy a drink. But, don't kid yourself. If you are looking for a job, the British can be extremely cold, rude and brutal.

Some of it may be the result of penny-pinching from the managerial brigade who know the cost of everything but the value of nothing. But, in my view, it is simply shoddy public relations. The person trying to get a job today, may be a client of tomorrow and his or her attitude towards a company will have changed because of the poor way in which an application has been handled.

I applied for close to 100 jobs in the 18 months between learning of my redundancy and finding a job. I failed to get past the first stage of the process in around 90 per cent of them. That was depressing enough, although probably par for the course for many over-50s looking for work. But I certainly remember the names of the companies who did not even bother to reply to the application I had spent several hours putting together. I don't buy their products and I don't pay to read their newspapers or websites.

A friend, who has won awards for his journalism, explained to me that some sports editors, who had previously spoken to him for years, simply ignored his emails looking for work after he was made redundant. I also experienced little warmth from editors when I was looking for a new start. I got the feeling that my time was gone in my early fifties and that my achievements in the past counted for nothing.

Not every organisation is like this. I take my hat off to one major trade union who sent me a rejection letter by post which was signed by the HR manager – the anti-thesis of the absent email. Surprisingly, some organisations which do not have massive staff, keep you in touch with the status of your application.

But you need to get used to the fact that generally there is little politesse in finding a job these days. Expect to be ignored and develop a thick skin in order to handle it. Assume you will not get a reply, if you have failed. Assume people are going to be ruthless. That way you are protecting yourself from getting angry from the indifference and lack of manners.

It is like driving in a busy city. There is no point expecting people to be polite behind the wheel. They are usually only interested in where they are going and they want to get there as quickly as possible. You simply don't matter. Now and again, however, somebody will wave and let you through in busy traffic. It is a surprise but a pleasant one on the road. Take the same attitude and adopt the same psychological tactics to your job seeking. Now and again, you will meet a polite employer with a human attitude to its recruitment process.

It is also important not to analyse your failure to progress too intensely. There were scores of jobs for which I thought I was well qualified where I did not even get an interview. And a few which I thought I had little chance of getting, where I was interviewed and went close to being offered the role. Sometimes there is little logic in the whole process, so a good tactic is not to analyse it too much.

What is crucial is that you deal with rejection in a way which does not stop you carrying on your search for a new start. From my days playing sport, I learned that the way somebody handles failure says more about that person than the way he or she deals with success. Anybody can handle success. Failure is much tougher.

All top sports performers have days when things go wrong and they lose, sometimes miserably. Few people in sport, business or life are successful all the time. So after rejection, pick yourself up, dust yourself down and keep running. Carrying too much anger on your shoulders from the whole process just slows you down.

This is where it is a good idea to put yourself in the position of the employer. I once applied for a job where I had been informed off-the-record by insiders that the management was keen to appoint a woman because the team was too male-dominated.

I learned how they had approached a female colleague with less experience than me and encouraged her to apply. I was not approached in the same way, even though people knew I was looking for a move. I decided to apply anyway and made it through to the second stage of interviews.

In the end, I did not get the job and a woman was appointed. I am not saying she was more or less qualified than me. Of course, employers are not allowed by law to discriminate against people because of their sex and I am sure that the organisation involved would say that they chose the best candidate and there was certainly no discrimination. I have no proof to suggest that is incorrect and the candidate who got the job is excellent.

But, rightly or wrongly, I did have a feeling that the tide was probably against me because of my chromosomes and it was going to be tough to swim against it. I was disappointed, of course, that I did not get the job because I felt I had performed well in the interviews, I met almost all of the requirements, and I could have done the job well. But, I then put myself in the position of the editor and understood that it was a good for him that he was able to balance his team in terms of gender representation. It was great for him that the best candidate was female.

Quite frankly, I would probably have done the same. I am a great supporter of getting more women into sports journalism and it is very much part of my efforts in the university field these days. Many woman would say that there has been discrimination against them in journalism for decades and they are probably right. I am proud of guiding some really good young female reporters into the profession in the last few years or so and helping to change that.

But I have to say that, I did get the feeling that my chromosomes did not help me much in that application process and it was bitterly disappointing at the time. What I am also saying is that applying for a job is a very complex business which is almost impossible to analyse correctly.

For example, it is also important to realise that decisions are not just taken on ability but also on how you might fit into the structure of an organisation.

One chief executive, who hired people regularly and held a high-profile position in sport, once told me: "You need to understand that people are hired on whether they fit into your team, rather than whether they have all the skills. If you are too senior and experienced, you may not fit into a younger team, for example. So don't beat yourself up about failing. Stop analysing it too much and move on to the next application."

This is excellent advice. If you feel you have put together a good CV and cover letter which meets the requirements of the job, then do not try to analyse why you have been rejected. It is pointless. If you can get some feedback, that is useful, but also bear in mind that companies cannot always tell all of the truth because of the law.

Often companies have already identified a preferred candidate and they are just "fishing" by advertising the job to see what sort of other candidates are on the market. Sometimes employers specifically want somebody younger than you – or older – and you just do not fit their needs. And, as I have explained, sometimes you have the wrong combination of chromosomes. Companies might have an ideal candidate in mind and you simply don't match up.

Some organisations also need to tick boxes in their recruitment. There are many arguments about whether this is positive or negative but there is no doubt that some professions do need more women, more people with disabilities and a better ethnic mix in order to reflect society. It is possible that you may tick no boxes at all and that could hinder your progress.

In politics, for example, a key way of changing the make-up of parliament in the UK has been to have all-women short lists for prospective members. I support this because sometimes the only way to make major changes is to be radical. This is allowed under Government legislation. But, of course, there will also be excellent young male candidates in a constituency who miss out because of the process.

The most frustrating rejection for me was when I knew that I was seriously being considered for a role but was unable to get the job over the line. Shortly after I was made redundant, I was approached by a senior editor at the Evening Standard newspaper who was looking for a new editor to oversee the sports coverage of the Standard, the Independent and the group's TV operation. I was well qualified because I had experience across newspapers, the web and TV and it was suggested to me that they wanted somebody with plenty of fresh ideas for the digital age.

I was asked to draw up a detailed plan of how I felt the group could improve its coverage to deal with the rapidly changing world where social media and the internet were replacing print as the main vehicle for serving up news to the public. I was then invited to a meeting at the elegant 19th century Gore Hotel near the Royal Albert Hall for a meeting with three senior editors about the job. In the media world, people love these kind of clandestine meetings at five-star hotels away from the office. I was asked about my interest in an assistant sports editor's job at the Mail on Sunday in the tea room of a similar plush hotel in Kensington where both the Evening Standard and Daily Mail group (Associated Newspapers) have their offices. I was once tapped up about a senior job at the Daily Telegraph in the bar of The Grosvenor Hotel near Victoria Station in a meeting arranged by the sports editor and his boss.

So I went to the Gore Hotel with a certain amount of confidence that I was being considered as a serious candidate. Sitting on a leather sofa with a gin and tonic with ice and lemon in my hand, I attempted to persuade the editors that I was the person for the job. The meeting seemed to go well and they listened attentively to my ideas. I came away thinking that I had a decent chance of getting the job. Then the wait began.

It seemed an age before anybody contacted me – it often does when you are out of work. In the end I was not offered the job or any role in the new structure. Of course it was disappointing but it was also immensely frustrating, knowing that I wasn't that far away from what would have been a really interesting chance to use the varied skills across the media which I had developed over the years.

I decided not to analyse the whole experience too closely because there were likely to be loads of reasons for the rejection but it took several weeks to get over the feeling of disappointment because I did have real hope of landing that job.

It is naïve, however, to think that anything is going to be easy in the job-hunting world. It can be a long slog to get over the finish line. So try to be practical and pragmatic about the rejections you face.

Most importantly, remember looking for a job is a numbers' game. You need to apply for jobs in which you are intere sted, of course, but you also need to get plenty of applications in. Always having an application being processed is also a good way of feeling that you are doing something about your situation. I always felt better when I pressed the submit button on an application.

If you do get rejected, feel disappointed for a moment but try not to analyse your failure too much and get on with the next application. As a friend of mine said to me: "It takes just one conversation to change the course of your life." You could be just one application away from that conversation.

Top 3 Tips:

Develop a thick skin and don't let a lack of replies to applications upset you.

Don't analyse rejection too much – you don't have all the facts at hand.

Keep going – it only takes one conversation to change your life.

10. WHEN SUCCESS COMES ALONG

Tasting the joy of making ground in your job-hunting.

Experiencing the joy of your business growing.

Getting new qualifications.

In April 2015, the tide turned for me at last. After a year of hunting for a permanent job, the call came from the Head of Culture and Communications School at the University of Bedfordshire. The presentation and interview for a senior lecturer's role in journalism had gone well earlier in the day. But that was also the case with an interview at a major London university a few months previously and I hadn't got the job. So I wasn't taking anything for granted.

"We would like to offer you the role," Professor Alexis Weedon said. Eight words that I had been chasing hard for a year. The campaign to get a new job had started before I left the BBC. After all the disappointments, despair and anger, my first feeling was one of sheer relief. It was only in the next few days that I realised how much tension I had felt for more than a year through the redundancy process and the unemployed period. Simply, because for the first time in a year, I felt relaxed.

It is true that my health had suffered during that period. I had tried to keep myself fit but, in late 2014, I had to undergo surgery to remove a painful gall bladder which kept me grounded for several months. Also my blood pressure was found to be way too high – certainly not helped by the stress of the redundancy and job-hunting. Now I needed to stop worrying for a while.

The university job was part-time (3 days a week) but I wanted it that way. It gave me more time to pursue my freelance work. And, after months of building up contacts and applications, the journalism jobs were also starting to stack up.

I had a place on the news service team to report from the European Games in Baku in Azerbaijan throughout all of June 2015, work in August at an Equestrian Olympic test event in Rio de Janeiro, Brazil and a two-month role reporting from the Rugby World Cup in England in the northern hemisphere autumn.

Many sports competitions these days run their own news service teams who provide detailed quotes from all the competitors before and after the games or tournaments plus news stories and features about the events. The details of these interviews are provided to all the journalists at the event who cannot be everywhere at the same time. For example, if you are covering an Olympic Games or a Rugby World Cup on your own, you can only go to one press conference or one event or game at a time and you need to know what has happened at other sports or matches and at other press conferences. One person cannot interview every athlete, so the journalists use the quotes and stories provided by the news service to enhance their work. The stories and quotes are also used on official websites for the event.

This was largely a new industry to me but I recognised it as a great opportunity to play some role in journalism. I had come across news services at Olympic Games before but I had never worked for one. To my delight, I was to find out that they are full of very experienced journalists, many of whom I knew. Some of them, I discovered, were in the same place as me in life – made redundant after years at their papers but wanting and needing to carry on reporting. Others were younger journalists keen to experience the magic of an Olympic Games but equally as professional and hard-working. The big positive was that the journalists were from all over the world and there was a multi-lingual camaraderie amongst them. I have enjoyed that because it reminds me of my days working at the international news agency Reuters where I relished the multi-national environment.

I cannot make a living solely out of working for these services but they have become an important part of my "portfolio" of work. More and more people in the UK are choosing to organise their careers in this way – carrying out a series of contracts to do different work for different employers.

Initially, I had not chosen this route, known as "portfolio working" at the start of my job-hunting but I soon realised it was the right way for me to organise my career at this stage of life.

The major advantage, in my opinion, is that you are not beholden to one person or one company. I had made the big mistake of thinking that the BBC would look after me, if I did a good job for them. In that way, I had trusted the organisation and put my career in the hands of the editors and managers.

It was a big mistake, they had shown me the door and I was determined not to make the same error again. The best way to do that is to have a handful of clients and activities. In that way, if you lose your job, you have more options. It is true that you have less security, in so far as you need to keep looking for new clients, but you also have more control over your life.

The university part of this is crucial because it provides the basic earnings plus pension from which I can develop the other activities. I have recently moved to Northampton University on a similar contract. I would not rule out taking a full-time job there, if I were to be offered one. But I would always make sure that I kept up some of the other journalistic activities. That is not a criticism of the university. I have a great set of colleagues but experience has shown me that you have to set up some safety nets in the 21st century workplace. I worked without a safety net at the BBC and it hurt when I fell.

Actually most progressive university journalism departments see outside activity as being important because you are gaining experience in an industry which is changing every month with developments in social media and multimedia. If you are still working in the trade, you can advise and guide students much better than somebody who is lecturing about how it was in their day. In 2019, the industry can change quite dramatically in a matter of months, so keeping up to speed with new developments is vital.

In April 2015, I was at the start of this journey into a new world. Don't believe I wasn't worried about adapting to it but I was also excited. The reality was that, apart from the odd guest lecture at a handful of universities, I had no experience of the higher education system. This was a completely new area and I knew I had a lot to learn.

In the next three years, I did just that – both in the job and in studying for a year (in addition to my lecturing) for a Postgraduate Certificate in Teaching in Higher Education (PGCTHE). I also became a Fellow of the Higher Education Academy, the body which promotes high-level teaching in UK universities. Gradually I began to feel at home in the academic world --- something I would never have thought I would a decade previously.

I was also able to develop not only freelance work writing for news services at major events including the 2016 Rio Olympics and Paralympics but also a new line of work teaching media skills to senior National Health Service (NHS) doctors and academics. I was broadening my skills and experience and moving more and more away from my old job of reporting for one organisation.

You can achieve this in your area. The basic lesson is that it is a "building exercise", brick-by-brick over a couple of years. The world will not change overnight after your redundancy but you can change it over 12 to 48 months if you keep your head up looking for different roles and your chin up too when things are not going so well.

Do not believe for one minute that you cannot do something different with your life. You can, if you develop your skills in the new area and show determination to make the contacts which will make that happen. Success and happiness can come out of the hardship of a redundancy, if you just keep going at many of the activities I have mentioned in this book.

Sometimes, just when you think you are getting nowhere, something will fall into your lap. In January 2017, a personal friend of mine recommended me to carry out some media training for an excellent company called Eden and Partners which works with NHS doctors and senior medical staff. They needed a trainer at the last minute for a course in Sheffield and I stepped in.

Since that day's work, I have been asked to take part in multiple courses with Eden and have enhanced my knowledge of the health sector and my experience in media training. Of course, I did my best to do a good job when the opportunity came along but I also owe my friend Elizabeth a few drinks, obviously, for helping me.

So success can come, if you keep trying and never give up. You can't win the lottery if you don't buy a ticket. So keep going with applications, networking and contacting possible clients.

Top 3 tips:

Always believe that success will come with time. Giving up is not an option.

Throw your heart and soul into any interesting opportunity.

Be prepared to study for new qualifications or take on different roles. You will enjoy the challenge.

11. REFLECTIONS

How to take time to reflect on your progress and "sniff the breeze".

Five key areas to consider.

Relishing your friends.

In the university world, academics love reflection. Reflecting on how the teaching went for you and your students, how your learning is going, how the research project is progressing. I once did a masters-level qualification where I was asked to "reflect on my reflection" as part of an assessment. I was lost at first and unsure what I was supposed to be reflecting about.

As a result, I have a mixed view on reflection. I think it is an important to look in the mirror now and again and reflect on how your career is progressing. But I do not believe it is healthy to spend too much time looking in the mirror and worrying about everything in your working life.

If you look at a tiny blemish on your face in the mirror every day, it will eventually seem much bigger than it really is because you are spending too much time focusing on it. In the same way, it is important to think now and again about whether you are getting what you want out of your career. But, whatever you do, avoid spending too much time reflecting. It is unhealthy.

This book, I hope, has made you think about how you can change the direction of your career but I would not recommend worrying about things every day. It provides, of course, several moments to reflect. But you also need to get on with living your life as well. Analyse now and again but don't analyse everything every day.

I try to put aside an hour a week to think about how things are progressing. I usually carry out this job with the dog. She walks through the fields with her nose to the ground most of the time and enjoys the exciting smells everywhere whilst I ponder about what I need to do in my working life. We are both sniffing the breeze really.

I have yet to reach a perfect situation, so there is always something to think about doing. You don't, of course, have to buy a dog to do this but take a walk in the fresh air, if you can, or go for a run, cycle ride or swim and do some thinking.

As I reflect on my life and career, four to five years after my redundancy, there are loads of positives and negatives. I suspect they are the same kind of themes that you have in your life, so I have put them into five different sections in this chapter, so that we can work on them together.

1.   *MONEY*

I am not earning as much money as I did as a salaried employee at the BBC four years ago. This is obviously a negative. I have some regular income and pension contributions from my university teaching but I have to keep working hard to ensure contracts come in for my freelance business. This has financial implications.

Try borrowing money from a bank on freelance income and you will probably struggle a bit. Most banks like to lend money based on guaranteed income and freelance work is never guaranteed. In general, I am therefore worse off financially than I was four years ago.

However, getting angry or frustrated about this is not going to do any good. I have plenty of colleagues who have set up their own businesses and are earning more than they did as an employee. The reality is that it can take time to build up a business, so I have to be patient about this.

As long as your general bills are covered by your income and you can have a reasonable life with the odd holiday, do not bother comparing your income now to what it was five years ago. Look at the quality of your life and reflect on whether you have more control over it.

If your relations with colleagues in a new job are better than your previous job, that is less stress and a better situation. This is all much more important than money. And, with time, you may be able to increase your income as your business grows or your new career progresses.

2. CONTROL

The more we feel in control of something, the happier we generally feel. As the pilot of a plane, you feel much more confident of arriving in a place safely than you do as a passenger where you have to put yourself in somebody else's hands. So control over your career and life is very important.

Four years ago, my career was very much in the hands of line managers at the BBC. Their decisions had a huge impact on my life and when they decided to make me redundant in my fifties, I had little choice but to put up with it. I have explained in this book, how unhappy this made me feel and how difficult it was to find another job.

The frustration of doing an excellent job for an organisation but still being shown the door is something I will never forget. So now having more control over my future is crucial to me. Of course, I am affected by decisions taken by bosses at the university where I am employed but my portfolio work means I have other options if they decide to show me the door.

In my freelance work, I deal with different clients. If I don't like working for them or they don't pay on time, I don't go back to them and I move on to other clients. I control much more of the jobs I carry out. In that way, this is a positive development overall because I am not beholden to line managers who can end my career with a click of their fingers, as I was at the BBC.

This could be important to you too. Could a different job make you more independent? Can you find a way to have more control over the rest of your life? Believe me, you will feel happier with more control.

3.   *FLEXIBILITY*

I used to think I was quite a flexible operator in journalism. I had worked for an international agency, a newspaper and in broadcasting, so I was used to providing reports in many different ways for papers, TV, radio and online.

I speak two foreign languages fluently, so I could work internationally as well as nationally and I published two books before this one. So compared to many journalists, who have not worked across different media, I was a very flexible worker.

The reality is, though, I have much more flexibility and adaptability now. I have needed to be more adaptable to survive. Before, I spent most of my days in the linear activity of researching a story and producing it in written or audio-visual form for newspapers or TV and radio. My skills were employed in a very ordered and simple way. Of course, there was some creativity but that came in the language, the choice of visual material and the reporting.

Now I need to be creative in so many different ways – from securing a contract with a client to carrying out a much wider range of work.

I teach students about journalism but I also report and write stories for clients and organisations, advise doctors and executives on how to deal with the media and I am constantly thinking up creative other ways of using the skills I have to make a living.

I am much more aware of how to sell my skills and how to run a small business. In the last four years I have been forced to get my head around key financial matters such VAT, invoicing, cash-flow issues and how to be persistent about chasing money from a client in a polite and positive way. More importantly, I am much more confident about taking on something new that I used to be.

Of course, journalism involves going into places every day which are new – and sometimes dangerous – as well as dealing with people whom you have never met before. But I was always doing a job I had done before.

Now I have to think on my feet and take on situations and roles which I have never carried out before and I am not afraid of that.

Setting up my own sole trader business has really helped me to develop in that way. You too can learn the same sort of skills by heading off into a new area and you will almost certainly have much more confidence to take on tasks that you have never done before. Never be afraid of that.

It is fine to be nervous but nerves should never stop you trying something. Change can be scary but it usually ends up being positive for our character and confidence.

4.   *CHARACTER*

Other people judge our character but I think (as much as I am allowed to judge my own character), I have developed a lot as a person in the years since my redundancy.

I would like to think that the experiences I have had – some good, some bad – have helped me to grow as a person. See, it can be possible, even for oldies like me.

The experience of having to go to a Job Centre for the first time for many decades to apply for benefits has given me a more grounded view of the world. I have always believed in social justice and helping people who have fallen on difficult times. I believe our taxes should be spent on key issues such as that.

But I have much more understanding of the stresses many people face when their jobs are in danger. Every time I hear news of a plant closing or a company being moved to another place, I know there are thousands of people facing the same emotions and difficulties which I had to endure.

Many will struggle to find a job because their skills may, at first, seem hard to transfer to another role. This is one of my main motivations for writing this book. If, by writing it, I help a few people have the confidence to make some important changes to their life, then I am happy.

I also believe I am better at working with people than I used to be. The fact that I have to work with many more people with different clients and at different locations has helped me to develop more skills at improving relations with colleagues.

I think I am happier in the workplace these days despite all the challenges I have faced. Clients have commented on my humour and good relations, so I hope that warmer and more composed attitude is seen by others.

By facing redundancy and then switching to a new role in life, it is almost inevitable that your character will develop for the good. You will have to think up ways of fitting into new environments and, although this may be challenging (especially if you have spent many years in the same organisation or office), you will learn a great deal from the experience.

You will also have to find ways of dealing with the ups and downs of hunting for a job. That will make you a better person. As I say in the chapter on rejection, you learn a lot about a person when they face failure. Anybody can deal with success.

You also develop a lot in your character when you face failure or rejection. It may not feel like it at the time but the way you have to pick yourself up and keep going will make you a better person in the long term.

5.   *FRIENDS*

There is no doubt you will learn who your close friends really are when you face redundancy. You will have some friends and colleagues who, as I have mentioned in the colleagues' chapter, will find it difficult to know what to say to you and will end up being strangers.

But you will also have plenty of friends who come to your rescue and provide you with important support as you make changes to your life. Some friends will help you to find other work -- that was certainly the case with me.

One of the most sobering lessons I learned through the whole process is that you are equally as likely to get work through the contacts of a friend or a colleague than you are by applying for a position. So the role of friends could be crucial for you in the job hunting.

But it is all important psychologically too. Don't be afraid of asking friends for advice. Don't assume they will know how you feel and, if your friends are willing to sit and listen to your woes, take up their offer of help and tell them how you feel.

It is often said that men are much worse at speaking to each other than women are. I think that is true to a certain extent. I believe women are much better at just listening to other women whilst men tend to be constantly trying to find solutions for their friends and partners.

That is the subject of another book from somebody much more qualified in human behaviour than me. But I know that sometimes people just need friends to listen, rather than give them a solution.

So, find somebody who will just listen to your troubles and feelings. Don't make it one-sided and ensure you listen to their troubles too. But sharing your emotions with a good friend is very important because it gives you the opportunity to download your troubles.

Eventually your meetings will involve fewer complaints and more fun and you will be able to share your progress towards change in your life with your friends. But, try if you can, to find some people who can help you through this process. I have a few friends who have stepped in with crucial advice along the way. They provided me with a perspective on the whole situation that I did not always possess.

You will make new friends and discover new qualities in other friends throughout your redundancy and career changes. Don't focus on the people who have turned into strangers. Cherish your new relationships.

12. BEING READY FOR NEXT TIME

Why everybody needs to have a Plan B to insure against redundancy.

The three stages of being ready for change.

Building up a contingency fund to feel confident and relaxed about the future.

The day I was called into an office at New Broadcasting House to be told by BBC bosses that I was being made redundant, one thought went through my mind for hours.

It stayed in my head for weeks and months afterwards. And now and again, it still taps the inside of my head and reminds me that I must not forget it. It is one simple question: "Why did I not do more to prepare for this situation?"

The reality is that I did see some of my redundancy coming on the horizon. My boss had hinted that cost-cutting was going to be tough and that I should not turn down any offers for other work. What I didn't see coming was the BBC turning its back on me and showing little willingness to find a new role for me in the organisation. Naïve, perhaps, but an understandable stance, given that it had been recognised at many levels that I had done an excellent job for them.

I remember how 10 o'clock News anchor Huw Edwards took me aside during the Olympics, praising my work and saying it had been noticed at higher levels. I had also received an assurance right at the time of my interview for the job in 2007 that everything would be fine for me once the Olympics were over. I had specifically asked the question about my job after the Games because I was giving up a better paid role at the Evening Standard to join the BBC. It was a risk and I was told clearly by one senior network editor that I would have few problems in the BBC, if I had made a success of the Olympics job. How wrong she was.

Perhaps my biggest mistake was that I had put my faith in the BBC to show loyalty. This has turned out to be the biggest error of my working life.

I did receive some help from my line manager with setting up one meeting in London and a senior editor in another department did help me with organising discussions with editors in Salford where BBC Sport and Radio 5 Live are based. But there wasn't much interest in my work and ideas and the meetings came to nothing, as did my applications for other jobs in the BBC. I certainly got the feeling that the BBC wanted me to walk out the door and never come back. Apart from one interview on Radio 4 and a few concerts with my choir on Radio 2 and 3 and at the BBC Proms, I have largely done that.

So the key lesson from this -- for any employee anywhere -- is to be prepared to be shown the door at any time, even if you are performing well and being praised regularly. Make sure you are ready – both psychologically and financially.

That sounds a bit dramatic, doesn't it? But actually it is not such a negative approach to life as it initially sounds. Keeping your options open and carrying out research about your next career move is a sound policy which will keep you on your toes and make you feel much more comfortable about your career.

I have friends who have done this and been very successful. Both were working as journalists but realised that were going to need to find another career in the next few years and started preparing for the day. One eventually faced a very quick redundancy while the other took the decision to leave an organisation at his time of choosing. But both of them spent about two years preparing for the journey.

One studied for a qualification in public relations and spent time talking to people in the communications industry. Eventually he was ready to take up a job at a major PR agency and resigned from his reporting job. He had made the contacts, understood the challenges and was ready for the move.

The other spent two years having conversations with an array of people about going into public relations or PR at the same time as carrying on with his work as a reporter. When the day came and his newspaper made him redundant in a matter of weeks, he did not take long to get a job in communications. He had prepared the way. He was ready too.

I wish I had prepared in the same way. I will never make the same mistake again. Now I think regularly about whether I need to change direction again. That does not mean I am not doing a good job for the organisations who employ me. It does not mean that I am not enjoying the work or putting in the right commitment. But it does mean I am having conversations with people and thinking about other options.

You don't have to have faced redundancy to think about all this. I would give this advice to everybody in work. Even if you are happy in your job, always think of a Plan B and have conversations with people. You don't need to say you are looking for a move. That might not help your business or that of your organisation. But getting advice and networking for the future is a positive way of giving yourself a safety net, if difficult days come your way. If you are a tightrope walker, you are not expecting to fall off but you are still much happier that there is a safety net below you. It is important for your wellbeing.

Maybe you have complete faith in your employer at the moment – and there is nothing wrong with that. It is not always misguided. But you will feel more comfortable if you know that you have other options, if things go wrong. And they can go wrong very quickly. A new boss might come in, the company might be taken over by a different firm with different objectives and policies, or outside factors, such as the state of the economy or your industry, might put strains on your workplace. And the ageing process sometimes puts you in a much more precarious position at work, even if age discrimination is against the law in most countries. Being over 50 in the media certainly does not feel comfortable, in my opinion. I fear that is a global phenomenon too.

If you have done your groundwork, you will be ready for a change. My friend's decision to carry out some extra studying was a very constructive one. I remember talking to him before he left his journalism job. He was enjoying the learning and feeling good that he was doing something positive about his future at a time when he was not enjoying his job.

There are three stages for this networking and preparation. The first stage is just talking to people about their experiences in other fields and thinking about what else you might want to do. The second stage is actively improving your position to get a job in that field through extra studying and conversations targeted at learning about the improvements you will need to make. And the third is asking people if there are openings since you want to switch jobs.

I would recommend working hard on the first stage for anybody in a job. You may never move to stage two or three but you will feel more comfortable knowing that there are other opportunities out there, if you needed or wanted to change jobs.

At the same time as you are doing this, I would recommend working on building up some savings which would pay the bills for six months, if you lost your job or wanted to do something different. As I have said in the chapter on money, this is not the same sum as six months of your salary now. It is likely to be a lot less because you are probably capable of living on less money. Set up a small account which is your "safety net cash" and contribute a little bit every month. Don't miss out on family holidays because of this fund but be disciplined in putting away an amount which is practical for you. Maybe take something out of your life (eg coffees and lunches bought at work) and put the funds into your special account. Before long, it will have accumulated enough money for you to survive for six months, if you lost your job for any reason. This may never happen but, you will feel happier knowing that you are covered financially, if it does.

If you work on these issues, you should be psychologically and financially ready for any turmoil in your career. Your safety net will be in place.

I wasn't ready in either way when I was made redundant and I regret that now. Learn from my errors and make sure you are.

Top 3 Tips:

Always be thinking about how you can change direction in your career.

Build up six months of emergency funds in order to survive sudden change forced upon you.

Be constantly building up your network of contacts to help with exploring new avenues.

THE FUTURE

In March 2018 I was invited into the BBC to be a guest on a live Radio 4 arts programme called *Front Row* with the talented presenter Kirsty Lang.

It was an unusual invitation and the first time I had returned to New Broadcasting House near Oxford St in central London since I was shown the door four years previously following the bizarre and depressing meeting in the Alan Partridge room which I describe at the start of this book.

It was unusual because the invitation had nothing to do with my seven years as a TV and radio correspondent at the BBC but more to do with my friends and freelance work since I had left. Unusual because it was about music – a leisure pastime for me, not a profession. And unusual, because it is the only time I have done any broadcasting in five years since I was forced out of the BBC.

I was asked to speak about the importance of theme tunes for sports programmes in the 1970s following an article I wrote about them for the culture section of the Telegraph website in 2015. If you are a middle-aged man or woman in the UK – and in some other countries -- you will remember the music of *Grandstand, Match of the Day, The Formula One theme, Test Match cricket and Wimbledon,* some of which are still being used today. They were almost all fanfares -- with plenty of trumpets involved --- calling sports fans to their television sets and they made a huge impact.

It is hardly a subject of great academic depth, but a producer had found my article about them in a search through the Internet. Unlike newspaper cuttings, which usually end up at the bottom of bird cages, stories on the web can be around forever. This means they can still get you work years after you write them.

The main reason I had penned the Telegraph article was that I was singing with Crouch End Festival Chorus at the inaugural Sports Prom at the Royal Albert Hall that year and Culture Editor Martin Chilton, who used to be my Sports Editor at the Evening Standard, asked me for a piece. He knew I had been made redundant and needed the work.

Four years on *Front Row* was interested in sporting tunes from the past because American composer Brian Tyler, who was also a guest on the programme, had just written a new theme for Formula One, aimed at a global market.

The reason I mention all this in detail is that the whole scenario sums up a lot of what I have been trying to say in this book about changing your life and how friends, colleagues and contacts are crucial in helping you along the way. You need them as much – or even more – than an ability to fill in an application form and search the right websites for jobs.

There was a certain symmetry in returning to the scene of one of the darkest days of my career. But I was in a completely different place now – teaching at a university and running a freelance journalism business. Life was certainly better than it was in the Alan Partridge room, I thought, as I walked out of

BBC HQ towards Great Portland Street underground station. It was a familiar five-minute walk that I had taken every day for seven years but it now had a very different feel.

I am not suggesting this is an amazing success story – it certainly isn't. It is a very ordinary journey. But I hope this book is useful to you because I didn't bounce back from redundancy to become a millionaire and household name. Far from it. That would have been unrealistic for most of you to emulate.

I followed a path to what I call "career survival" which many of you are capable of following in your fields, trades and professions. Ordinary but stimulating. Emotional ups and downs but eventually enjoyable. Sometimes frustrating but often rewarding. After a career of making headlines in TV, radio and newspapers, I had changed my life without getting into the news or making a lot of noise. It was a long, gruelling journey, sometimes lonely and often frustrating.

And how had I got there? Friends played a huge role. Firstly, I had spent the day before the Radio 4 evening broadcast teaching senior doctors and NHS medical staff how to handle the media in a special conference at Westminster – part of regular media training work I had secured with the respected company Eden & Partners through a personal friend's recommendation. Of course, I had to do the job well for the client but the initial contact was through my friend Elizabeth who also worked for the company.

Secondly, I was invited onto a radio programme thanks to an article I had written on the request of a former colleague and friend Martin who knew I was looking for work and wanted to help.

Overall, friends and former colleagues have played a big part in helping me to find work. They will be equally important to you. So, as I have said in the chapter about networking, make sure everybody you respect knows you are looking for work --- as soon as you are made redundant. When I worked on the images for the cover of the paperback version of this book, I made sure it had the image of somebody helping somebody else up. We all need a helping hand at some point in our lives.

As I have said many times, I believe getting a new job or changing your career is a multi-faceted exercise where you have to work on several fronts. In addition to networking and talking to friends and colleagues, you need to apply for jobs, update your CV, improve your education and try all the things I have mentioned in this book, if you can. Communication is a key part of this. Do not hide away. You need to get back on the street and work will eventually come to you.

What's next for me? The joy is that I don't know exactly. Of course, I hope to continue my university work teaching the next generation of journalists and I will work hard to keep my freelance business ticking over with writing, media training, conference-hosting and communications advice. I have plans for a book about journalism.

Are there moments when I miss my past role working full-time as a journalist? Of course, there are. I feel cheated out of a crucial last decade and a half of a career as a full-time campaigning, questioning reporter. When I was made redundant, I had plenty more to give to the profession to which I have dedicated most of my life. That is the source of my resentment. As I have said, I doubt those feelings of anger and frustration will ever go away completely but I do not have them every day or every week. They are locked away in a box on a top shelf and they only occasionally sneak out.

But I know that there are many people like me in my trade and in many other professions and businesses. There really is only one solution to this kind of frustration: If people are not willing to answer the door to you, stop banging your head against it and try knocking on different doors to happiness. I have and I am pleased to have met and worked with some wonderful people in the years since I was made redundant.

Who knows what is around the corner? I may find something else interesting where I can use the skills I have developed during my career to provide a totally new service for a client. I now have the confidence to try anything new and I have learned that my skills go way beyond the largely linear task of writing or broadcasting and chasing a news story.

In short, redundancy has turned me into a different person who is much more flexible, creative and streetwise – and, I hope, more understanding of the challenges which many people face every day trying to find a job.

I hope this book will help you on the same journey, remembering with every single step the valuable advice of my friend Kurt Barling that it "takes just one conversation to change your life". That conversation could be just around the corner in your next phone call, email or meeting. Make it, write it or arrange it.

Adrian Warner. May 2019

ABOUT THE AUTHOR

Adrian Warner is an award-winning sports journalist
who has spent 33 years reporting for Reuters,
London's Evening Standard newspaper and the BBC
as an on-screen TV and radio correspondent. He has
reported from 14 Olympic Games and five soccer
World Cup finals and from 25 countries, including a
decade as a foreign correspondent based in mainland
Europe.

Adrian is a Senior Lecturer in Multimedia Journalism
at the University of Northampton in the UK and runs
his own journalism, media training and
communications consultancy business. When he is
not teaching, writing or cycling, he sings for London's
Crouch End Festival Chorus and has performed live
with leading performers such as Ray Davies, Noel
Gallagher and Andrea Bocelli.

You can reach his website at
www.adrianwarnermedia.com

Printed in Great Britain
by Amazon